Tit For Tat Exchanges

We'll start our story with our hometown newspaper setting up shop next door to us. This sets into motion a Goldberg device chain of reactions whereby our lives corkscrew into controlled craziness.

Upon sharing our unique backstory, we are prompted to put pen to paper and publish.

Encouraged by our community we are destined not to be one of those one-hit wonders. On the contrary, the hits just kept on coming. Five years later we find ourselves cresting on the wave of having written a million words spanning three books and several hundred articles on a diverse array of topics including international adventures revolving around topics including entertainment, human interest, travel, sports and history.

So what exactly are you holding in your hands right now? These are the words that have brought the most laughter and the occasional tears to our regular readers. We look forward to adding you to our roster.

As we surpass the aforementioned million-mile marker in terms of the volume of our work, here are the 50,000 words that, as our subtitle specifies, comprise Tim & Deb's Greatest Hits.

Tit For Tat Exchanges

Tim & Deb's Greatest Hits

± ± ± ± ±

by

Tim & Deb Smith

Pandamensional Solutions, Inc.

Mendon, New York

Published by Pandamensional Solutions, Inc., Mendon, NY

Cover design by Catarina Carosa

ISBN-10: 1-938465-08-3
ISBN-13: 978-1-938465-08-6

What Others Are Saying About Tim & Deb Smith's
Tit For Tat Exchanges

"I often enjoy books like *Tit For Tat* that indulge my desire to simply dabble at reading. Rather than requiring my serious focus on characterization and complicated plotting, I was sampling entertainment and levity in short bursts, along with all the alliteration and limericks I could handle. I found the Smiths' tidbits covering all the information I never realized I needed to know both intriguing and quirky.

I kept thinking to myself, "They have to be making this one up!" only to be drawn to Google one more time being hooked in to find out more. "Scrumdiddlyumptious children", "bat satchels", "Froggyland"? It's all here, folks. As promised, they don't shy away from anything!

The Smiths do have a way with words that somehow harken back to earlier days of our lives. To rediscover it, you'll just have to read "the dadgum thing". It will all come back!"

~ Librarian Rhonda Jagnow

"The aspects of the Smiths' writing that makes this book for me is the incredible diversity of the content. I didn't know how much I didn't know. From Indian orgies to wet pussy willow whipping, it's all here.

My favorite chapter was the one on Endangered Babies. Every time I finished a segment I would laugh and think to myself, "This is the funniest damn baby story I have ever heard!" Then the next story would be even better. In general the Smiths' writing style rises to crescendos throughout this book. It makes for a great ride and I look forward to the day when "vomit slide" becomes part of our everyday lexicon.

This is one of those books that is going to make you look good because when you give it to your friends to read you come off looking like a total genius for being the one who has discovered these heretofore relatively unknown writers."

~ Dr. Frederick J. Marra

"Greetings from Christmas Island and it's lovely to hear from you! I have just read your book and it is fantastic. So much thought and attention to detail, certainly one of my favourite CI pieces of writing."

    ~ Christmas Island Tourism Director Jahna Luke

"Of the many jaw-dropping revelations in *Tit For Tat*, I'll pick one that I've not been able to rattle out of my brain. Right in the middle of the city in Bern, Switzerland there is a huge statue of an ogre eating babies. He's got one baby halfway down the hatch and three more queued up to complete his 4-course meal. It's just one of dozens of great stories."

    ~ Historian Mike McGory

Dedication

We must be willing to give up the life we've planned,
so as to embrace the life that is waiting for us.

TABLE OF CONTENTS

FOREWORD

By Educator Robert Caulkins

Like every opening of a *Goldberg*s episode, the year was 1980-something when I first met Tim Smith. I was a high school freshman and he was a high school English teacher. I was enthralled with his wit and humor; he connected stories about music and sports in much the same way as a plot line on *Seinfeld.*

Our relationship continued after high school where it grew to include road trips, festivals, professional baseball games, and concerts. From the Beach Boys to Buffett and all ports in between. It was always Five O'clock Somewhere.

My amazement with Tim was always about his passion and foresight. When VCRs came out, he constructed an incredible library of music videos and current and past TV shows. Tim was ahead of the rejuvenation in animation as well. He was incredibly innovative in teaching literary elements using cartoons. His expertise led him to being invited to speak at 1992 World Festival of Animated Films in Zagreb, Croatia. Besides Tim, who knew how educational Bugs Bunny could be?

At my 35th High School reunion I was able to meet Deb and witness firsthand what an amazing connection existed between the two of them. I'll let the book tell their remarkable story; it truly is one for the ages. This encounter led to my reading of their first book *The Beatles, The Bible & Manson.* Tim and Deb's writing style and thorough research led to attending a book talk at a local library, and my interest in their work completely solidified.

While reading *Tit For Tat* I was taken on a magical mystery tour of the world of Tim and Deb through their weekly columns. Their stories run the gamut of educational, hilarious, surreal and in some cases even somber. Only the talents of Tim and Deb Smith could create a book that references bombs on bats, ogre-eating babies, an NFL player visiting their house and Miss USA as a neighbor.

Engaging in their stories is more like having a conversation with them. They will give information and insert insights and humor throughout. The topics range from sports and music to historical hijinks and far off countries. After reading the book, you feel like you have experienced the hipper version of Jules Verne's *Around the World in 80 days* and a season of *On the Road* with Charles Kuralt all in one.

Thank you for allowing me to read the advanced copy. It was a great honor to be asked by you, and I am thankful for all the laughs, knowledge and insights your work and friendships have given me. Can't wait for the next Tim and Deb submission, knowing you and your work has enriched so many.

ACKNOWLEDGEMENTS

We write a weekly feature for our local paper the *Mendon-Honeoye Falls-Lima Sentinel* which services the southern suburbs of Rochester, New York. We get the whole back page and our weekly contributions check in at about 1,500 words. With the publication of this book our total word count for all of our articles and books now exceeds a million.

But we don't want to get too hung up on the numerology. There's always another superlative to put things in proper perspective. For example, there's a billion people in China. Do you know what that means? In China, if you are a one-in-a-million kind of guy, there's a thousand other guys just like you!

At any rate, recapping the story of our writing, the publisher of our newspaper, Chris Carosa, had been encouraging us for some time to write a book. While the idea always intrigued us, we didn't jump right on board because we were having too much fun on our foray flitting from one topic to another. In general, our column has covered an eclectic variety of topics including music, sports, travel, history and human interest.

The stars, for us, aligned in the beginning of 2019 when we connected the dots on some historical events and came to realize that occurring within a 30-day period that coming summer would be the 50th anniversaries of First Man on the Moon, Chappaquiddick, the Manson Murders, Woodstock and one other thing … it also happened to be the 50th anniversary of the day we met.

We were waiting for a sign from God and this seemed to be thrust down upon us like a lightning bolt hurled here from Heaven. We needed to pick one of those 50th anniversary events, take it by its literary horns and run with it. That led to the composition of our first book, *The Beatles, The Bible & Manson: Reflecting Back with 50 Years of Perspective*.

At this point, many of you may be wondering, "Why pick the Manson story?" Well, we actually have a pretty good answer for that. Think about the story potential for the anniversary options. Man on the Moon may have been the most tempting tale, but where do you go with the storyline? *"Rocket ship flies to the moon, dude gets out and walks around, dude climbs back into rocket and flies home."* Story over.

Regarding the Manson story, while it is obviously a totally tragic tale, it's truly intriguing. What with all the sex and drugs and rock n roll, the story has so many bizarre twists and turns it gets interesting even if you don't want it to be. Every time you turn a corner there's another "I can't believe it" moment. So that one worked out well and we're on to book two, which is the one you are now holding in your own sweet hands.

Please allow us to explain to you how we landed upon our title, *Tit For Tat Exchanges ~ Tim & Deb's Greatest Hits.*

Let's start at the end of the title and work our way forward. Our subtitle of Tim & Deb's Greatest Hits reflects the fact that this book showcases the most positively received features we have published over the past 5 years, thematically clustered.

The first half of the title is a reference to the single line we wrote that generated the greatest response from our readers. At one point we did a story on Easter Island and that piece did not make the book, so we're not going to be giving anything away by using our one titillating line from that story in the introduction here.

Easter Island is a territory of Chile located off the western coast of South America in the Pacific Ocean. One part of our Easter Island coverage featured a dispute between the territory of Easter Island and its mother country of Chile which was described as a tit-for-tat exchange.

We love to analyze and play with words and that storyline gave us pause to ponder ... isn't "tit-for-tat" such an interesting little colloquialism? Does not that pause to ponder give one cause to wonder, "What exactly is tat? How do I get some? And where can I turn it in for the other thing?"

As two former teachers we would like to jointly assume the role of that favorite teacher you had in high school. You remember the one. It was the teacher who demanded that you work hard, but you didn't mind doing the work because the class was engaging and you knew you would emerge not only educated but inspired.

So at this point please allow us to become your tour guides for a serendipitous sojourn. We will run you through the gauntlet of your total emotional spectrum. We will make you laugh. We will make you cry. And if things work out right, there will be a few occasions on which we'll make you laugh so hard you'll cry.

Surf's up. Let's do this!

Tim & Deb Smith
Mendon, New York
November 15, 2020

CHAPTER 1
STORYLINE SAMPLER

Welcome to our second book. It is our grandiose goal to enticingly engage you in a joyful journey through an amazing array of tantalizing topics. In establishing our objective, we sought to achieve the perfect balance of educating our audience as well as entertaining you. Please prepare yourself for an eye-opening and mind-expanding menagerie of research and revelations upon which we have wantonly worked for the past several years.

We are two retired school teachers who have honed our writing skills while composing the full-page feature which comprises the back page of our local paper every week. Just to play around with the numerology piece, we have written about a million words in our collective literary career and we are about to share with you, in this book, what we consider to be our best 50,000. It's *Tim and Deb's Greatest Hits,* so to speak.

But we realize that the numbers alone don't tell the whole tale. In the end it comes down to quality not quantity. Think of it this way. There are a billion people in China. Do you know what that means? If you live in China and you're a one-in-a-million kind of guy, there's a thousand other guys just like you. (Where have you heard this before?)

So in our quest to entertain you, we will not be restrained by the nuances of numerology. We plan to execute an overall style which runs the gamut of emotions. On occasion we hope to move you to tears, but for the most part we're haranguing for humor.

With that in mind we hereby offer up a first chapter sampler of what you can expect throughout this book. It will be our goal to entertain as well as educate you on a vast variety of topics. Our purpose having been thusly established, here's a sumptuous sampling of snickering snippets we hope leaves you tempted to turn some more pages.

PINK PANTIES - We spent Halloween 2018 at an Alice Cooper concert in Syracuse and it was a seasonally exciting experience. The last time we had seen the band was during our senior year in high school. One rite of passage that we will always be able to claim is that the ultimate Alice Cooper anthem "School's Out" was released during our senior year. The lyrics "School's Out Forever" resonated in our hallowed hallways as we cleaned out our high school lockers for the final time.

During those years, we enjoyed Alice Cooper's extreme eccentricities such as his androgynous look, female first name, and wild eye makeup; it was all part of the show. But we also remember our parents being skeptical of the whole thing and it was a skepticism that swirled through the psyche of the conservative Middle American subconscious.

Back in the day vinyl record albums were released with the record slid inside a paper sleeve for protection. The paper sleeve was, in turn, slid inside the album cover. In another example of how this band continually pushed the envelope, when it came to the record sleeve for the *School's Out* album, Alice Cooper purposefully passed on the paper and playfully put on the panties. The original release of the album featured the record slid inside a pair of pink panties rather than a sleeve of white paper.

We actually just checked for this on eBay and original *School's Out* albums, with the panties still in good condition, are selling for $250. That provided ample impetus for us to sally forth on a foray up to our antiquated attic and see if we could find our old original album. Fortunately the valuable vinyl was located intact, with panties. The doubly good news for us is that Deb only wore them a few times. What can we say? We were crazy kids.

FAREWELL TO A FALLEN FRIEND ~ Tim taught high school English for 33 years and it is not unusual for us to run into former students who are anxious to convey how impactful he was on their lives. In a related story, on the morning of July 3, 2017 we received an email informing us that Scott Reese, one of Tim's former students, was dying of cancer and his family reached out to us to see if we could use our connections to score tickets for him to see his favorite group, Tom Petty and the Heartbreakers, who were performing the following night in Canandaigua, New York.

Fortunately, we were able to come through for them, and the entire backstory is one of the few tear-jerking components of our book. What follows below is an inspired paragraph we wrote after having made all of the necessary arrangements with the outdoor venue director Heather, and walking up to the top of the hill to take it all in as we waited for Scott's arrival. As we contemplated the obituary, we knew we would soon be writing, the following paragraph formulated in our brains.

As the shimmering sun serenely sets on the summer shoreline, we watch the cacophony of cascading colors create a Canandaigua crescendo as they reflect off the water. "This is," Heather says, "one of my favorite things to do if everything down below is copasetic." As the three of us stand at the very top of the hill overlooking the lake it becomes a transcendent moment. The Seneca Indians bestowed the name "Canandaigua" upon this setting because, in their words, it meant "the chosen place." For this brief moment, frozen in time, there is a Great Spirit enveloping us with the realization that the Senecas chose wisely.

If you happen to have been connecting the dots on this timeline, you may have already realized the double irony of this storyline. Within two months Scott Reese and Tom Petty would both be dead. Always remember, you don't have to live like a refugee.

HIGH SCHOOL HILARITY ~ As we mentioned in the previous story, Tim taught high school English for 33 years and here is what he considers to be his funniest story from that teaching career. Shakespeare's *Romeo and Juliet* was a part of his curriculum every year. The go-to high school movie version of *Romeo & Juliet* has traditionally been Franco Zeffirelli's classic 1968 film which starred Olivia Hussey as the 14-year-old Juliet. A key point in the story occurs when Romeo and Juliet wake up after having spent their wedding night together.

Juliet was played by the amply endowed Olivia Hussey and, for a split second, when she gets up to say goodbye, her bountiful breasts spill out of her robe and, let's put it this way ... if the movie had been made in 3-D, some people in the front row could have been seriously injured. While the view lasts only a split second, for the 14-year-old boys in that classroom it was a second that may have lived on for hours, or days, or weeks.

When Tim was wrapping up class, he would usually close by asking if anybody had any questions. The end of class, on what became fondly remembered as the Day of the Bouncing Boobs, was always a little different with the kids kind of looking at each other waiting and wanting to say something about the risqué shot, but not knowing how to do it without coming off as crude or crass.

So usually nothing was said, the bell rang, and the kids went on their way. Only once in 33 years did one of Tim's 14-year-old freshmen perfectly thread the needle. Here's the favorite line of Tim's teaching career.

During the aforementioned end-of-class Q & A one freshman boy raised his hand, and in a casual reference to the buxomly bare-breasted Olivia Hussey scene proffered the question, "Mr. Smith, was Juliet really only 14 years old?"

PAUL IS DEAD? ~ Next, we will share with you what was one of our favorite concluding paragraphs. The topic of the piece was the 1969 hoax that Beatle Paul McCartney had died in a car accident and been replaced in the band by a lookalike. Of course, it wasn't true, but there was a few-month-long fall frenzy that year where the planet was perplexedly paralyzed by the preposterous proposition purported about poor, poor pitiful Paul.

Of course, adding an element of interest to this storyline was the fact that the Beatles collectively denied culpability in the collaboration of clues which fanned the fire fueling the hoax. That being said, those British boys are sometimes full of Irish blarney. Beginning with the *Sgt. Pepper* album in 1967 the preponderance of cleverly included clues seemed to confirm that the Fab 4 was having some fun with their fans, including us. We closed this piece with the following paragraph.

We were totally immersed in the frenzy when we were in high school and the story was initially breaking. As a matter of fact, the storyline overlapped precisely with the months that we were first dating, serving to create the perfect double bonus. It gave us something to talk about before we started having sex. That was a good thing because we've barely spoken to each other since.

SEXUAL FANTASIES ~ One of our most well-received pieces was when we created a game that people could play in their cars while traveling through Central Pennsylvania. Might seem like an odd pretense but there's a method to our madness. If you were to travel from Canada to Key West you could get from Niagara Falls to Key Largo without ever leaving expressways except for one 72-mile stretch in Pennsylvania. Because it is the only opportunity for commercial establishments to lure in potential customers without drivers having to take the expressway off-ramp option, the stretch is populated by a plethora of shops selling sordid sex, frenetic fireworks and Native American artifacts.

Sure, billboards are nice, but when Clyde Peeling's Reptile-Land is right there by the side of the road, don't the kids have a much better chance of talking you into a stop? And if you happen to make your way to the snack bar, here's our inside tip.

The café at Clyde's doesn't show up on Pennsylvania's list of five-star restaurants but, for what it's worth, we hear the deep-fried gator nuggets are to die for. At any rate, here is our opening paragraph for the feature that we titled "Deb & Tim's Totally Twisted Route 15 Fun Foray."

If you've ever fantasized about dressing up like an Indian and having sex under the fireworks then, for you, Route 15 south of Williamsport, Pennsylvania might just be a little slice of heaven right here on earth. Since we've just nailed your sexual fantasies to a "T", we're sure that some of you are wondering how we've managed to peek into your bedroom window or hack into your computer. Well, don't feel bad, the Indian fireworks thing has been on our Top 10 list for many moons.

CHAPTER 2
BIZARRE TALES OF ENDANGERED BABIES

After reading this title you're probably thinking, "Where in the world are they going with this one?" The answer would be to three places actually ... Castrillo, Spain; Bern, Switzerland; and Vilnius, Lithuania. As we continue to span the globe in our never-ending endeavor to inform and entertain, we are now bringing to you three tales so bizarre that if you did not hear them from a credible source you'd think, "No way is this true!" And perhaps the most bizarre part of this story so far is the fact that we just referred to ourselves as credible. Credibility notwithstanding, we'll take you to Spain first.

BABY JUMPING IN SPAIN

FESTIVAL OF EL COLACHO ~ If you have always had the desire to participate in a bizarre traditional Spanish ceremony, and running with the bulls in Pamplona seems a tad too dangerous for you, we have an alternative suggestion. It is the Festival of El Colacho, also known as the Baby Jumping Festival.

What does this festival have, you may ask, that the running of the bulls does not? Well, for starters, men dressed like devils swatting festival attendees with whips, forgiveness of original sin, babies laid out on rows of mattresses on the street, and for dessert let's throw some rose petals over the whole shebang. Perhaps the running of the bulls might suddenly sound like a more attractive alternative than you first thought.

All of this frivolity occurs at the annual Baby Jumping Festival in the small Spanish village of Castrillo de Murcia. And our #1 reason for you to read on is that, believe it or not, the Catholic Church is behind the whole damn thing. Before the era when the church was busying itself with issuing dictums on birth control and promoting Friday night fish fries, it had the time to conceive and sponsor the Festival of El Colacho, the original purpose of which was to cleanse babies of original sin.

Historical records indicate that this festive and frenzied family funfest originated around 1620, so the 400th anniversary has been celebrated. Here's the backstory ... six weeks after Easter, the Spanish begin a week of celebration known as Corpus Cristi. The Baby Jumping Festival occurs on the first Sunday after Corpus Cristi. You may want to pencil this in on your calendar right now so you won't forget.

Even if the concept seems sketchy, isn't it rewarding to know that those 17th century popes weren't just sitting on their robes, doing nothing? Their goal of adding family frivolity to the lives of young and futuristic religious zealots never eluded them but, oh my God, if you can do that while simultaneously cleansing original sin haven't you pretty much hit the papal jackpot of joy?

And for the Holy Trinity trifecta, doesn't the exhilaration of escaping near death as an infant no doubt heighten one's enthusiasm to return the blessing when that collection plate gets passed around somewhere down the road? But enough for the amusing musings, before the suspense kills you, let us cut to the chase and explain what happens at the Baby Jumping Festival.

NUTS AND BOLTS - Here is how the whole thing works ... anyone who has had a child born in the last year can place their infant on mattresses lined up in a series of rows. Think of it this way; if it were a track meet, the rows of babies would essentially equate to hurdles.

Pillows are provided free of charge. This provision is apparently based upon the notion that if you, as a parent, are willing to imperil your baby's life by letting total strangers jump over your child, certainly comfort is of tantamount importance to you. As the babies squirm, fidget, cry or giggle; the crowded throngs which have lined both sides of the street find themselves eerily violated.

DEVILS APPEAR - Emerging from hidden locations, men dressed in red and yellow devil costumes penetrate the crowd playfully striking random festival goers with toy whips. We know right now that a couple thoughts are running through your head ...

- #1) How can anything be this much fun before the main event has even begun? ... and
- #2) How can I get my own whip?

Once the crowd has been wistfully whipped to the devils' complete content and definitely driven into a fanatical frenzy, we anxiously approach the aforementioned headline attraction.

LET THE GAMES BEGIN ~ At this point the costumed devils assemble at the beginning of the parade route. Row upon row of unsuspecting babies lie before them, literally. One by one the devils start running, getting up a full head of steam, because the approaching rows of babies are not the kind of hurdles upon which one would want to come up short. If you can't feel the palpable tension in the crowd at this point, then you are clearly not a baby lover.

In perusing the pictures, we have seen of this event, and these can be viewed on the internet, we do have one safety suggestion we are going to send to the festival's directors. Could we not achieve the desired result of cleansing the babies' original sins if we lined them up with their feet at the **end** of the jump? That way if something were to go wrong, the leaping devil would step on the baby's toes rather than crush its skull. Just a thought.

FINAL FLOWERS ~ So much fun and it's not completely over yet. The crescendo of this festival focuses on the concept that everyone in attendance is allowed to participate in some way. If no one has whipped you or jumped over you so far, your opportunity to officially join the festivities has now arrived.

The grand finale of the Baby Jumping Festival is the spreading of rose petals over the surviving babies. At this point, all attendees who have brought their own rose petals are invited to become part of the final crusade. That congregation of flower bearers then walks the parade route showering their petals down upon the babies. And the world comes together as one.

THOSE WACKY CATHOLICS ~ As explained above, the centuries-old purpose of the Baby Jumping Festival is to cleanse the infants of original sin, essentially the same as baptism. So this establishes the original connection to the Catholic Church. While the Baby Jumping Festival was initiated with the most devout Catholic intentions, obviously times have changed and some of the antics that those wacky early 17ᵗʰ century Catholics could get away with have slid toward the opposite side of the scale of modern-day political correctness. That being said, there is no talk of discontinuing this festival, but in 2012 Pope Benedict did go so far as to encourage Spanish clergy to "distance yourselves from the ritual."

One thing we did in our first book, which people seemed to like, was that at strategic locations we included some limericks and other poetic verses. We'll initiate that motif here with one limerick from each of our endangered babies' stories. Here's how this one might look from the perspective of the babies.

> *At least things here never get dull*
> *With Devils a-dancin' there's never a lull*
> *Let the jumping begin*
> *Inform next of kin*
> *If these Devils from Hell crush my skull*

If babies being jumped over raised some concern on your part, definitely change a diaper and return for our next segments where you'll hear true tales of babies being eaten and raced. Not that you'll sleep any sounder but just so you know, the babies who are competing in the race are not the ones that get eaten. If the Grimm brothers can get away with "Hansel and Gretel", the Smiths can get away with this.

THE CHILD-EATER OF SWITZERLAND

The theme of this chapter's next part is the actual consumption of babies and, spoiler alert, the cannibal who stars in this show makes the witch in "Hansel & Gretel" look like a lightweight. Any ogre who wimps out and actually cooks the kids before consuming them earns no respect at all from The Child-Eater of Bern, in Switzerland. Here's the scoop, and we're not talking ice cream.

THE CHILD-EATER STATUE ~ If you ever want to scare the crap out of your kids take them to Bern, Switzerland to see the fountain statue of the Child-Eater. The statue, which was built in 1546, stands right in the middle of town and depicts a giant ogre, teeth bared, with a baby half stuffed into his gaping mouth.

This looks to be the appetizer in a four-course meal as the ogre has another baby cradled under his left arm and two more stuffed into a sack. The anguished looks on the faces of the uneaten children seem to be conveying the notion that they realize the invention of the baby monitor is centuries away from helping them out of this impending demise.

THE THEORIES ~ For any statue this bizarre, you would think that someone would have documented the reason for its creation, but surprisingly this is not the case. There are three theories floated about the inspiration for this questionable cuisine, none of which rise to the top as the clear favorite.

- It could be a depiction of Greek mythology. In that liturgy, Cronus was the leader of the first generation of Titans. As the story goes, he tried to devour all of his children in order to prevent his overthrow. But when Zeus managed to escape the hors d'oeuvre tray, the downfall of Cronus was imminent.
- The ogre's hat resembles a judenhuts which was required head gear for Jewish men of that era. This suggests a reference to the now debunked 16th century belief that Jews murdered children to use their blood for religious rituals.
- The last theory is that the statue depicts the brother of Duke Berchtold, who was the founder of Bern. The Duke's brother went crazy and the rumor at the time was that he supposedly ate some of the local children. There is, however, no historical evidence to support this theory.

BEARS CIRCLE THE BASE ~ And as if the whole concept of this statue is not already bizarre enough, there are eight bears, each armed with some kind of weaponry, marching in a circle around the base. Some of the bears are looking up as if they are observing the ogre ingesting the scrumdiddlyumptious children, hoping against hope that perhaps an appendage or two might fall their way.

Whatever the Child-Eater of Bern was originally meant to represent, the result we are left with today is the culinary nightmare of every kid in the world.

That fairy tale witch was a cheater
In kid-eating I know I'll beat her
It's clearly the law
You eat the kids raw
Or so says the Bern Baby-Eater

LITHUANIAN BABY RACING

EASTERN EUROPEAN ESCAPADES ~ Set your calendar. Every year on June 1st the world acknowledges International Child Protection Day. Depending on your individual schedule, you may, or may not, have missed the celebration of this one last year. But if you lived in Lithuania it would have been a whole lot harder to miss.

Every country has its quirky celebrations. Look in the mirror. Your country, the good old U.S. of A., celebrates the Coney Island hot dog eating contest every 4th of July. So, don't come down too hard when you hear that every June 1st Lithuania is totally caught up in a fervor of excitement over the annual Lithuanian Baby Races.

LOGISTICS ~ Here's how it works, as well as some highlights from previous competitions. The event was conceived in 1999 because no eastern European country wants to let a millennium slip away without showing how much wacky fun they've been having since achieving independence from the Soviet Union.

The race track consists of five yards of the plushest carpet the country has to offer, and it's laid out in four lanes. While the lanes are marked, there is no penalty for straying outside the lines; the first baby to cross the finish line is the winner, no matter how circuitous the route. You have one parent at the starting line and the other at the finish line.

Once the race begins parents are not allowed to make physical contact with their child, but they can coax and cajole by any other conceivable means. If you watch the videos of this on YouTube, you'll usually hear the parents calling their child, but the most successful means of persuasion seems to be the holding up and/or shaking of some physical object. A wide range of enticements have been employed including cell phones, favorite toys, baby bottles, balloons, key rings and basically anything flashy to lure their child across the finish line first.

ANYONE'S GAME ~ Certainly a great appeal of the race is its complete unpredictability. It's not uncommon for some of these tenaciously talented toddlers to sprint to an early lead and then fall flat on their faces, sometimes literally. Other times they charge right to the brink of the finish line only to become distracted or disinterested and come to a complete halt. Sometimes they go sideways. Some babies begin strong only to turn around and head back to the starting line. Some sit still and never cross the starting line. The possibilities are endless, which of course adds to the fun.

With dozens of annual entrants, logistics pretty much require that the overall champion is determined by the winning baby with the lowest time. If this were the Olympics the winners would be returned to the track for the next heat. But especially on International Child Protection Day that might be a little much.

THE RACE IS ON ~ Let us close by sharing with you what, by most accounts, was the greatest race ever. Let's set our Wayback Machine with the following coordinates . . . Location: Vilnius, Lithuania; Time: June 1st 2003. We've never had a chance to call a Kentucky Derby before, but we'll give our best shot to this opportunity to describe that race. As previously stated, four babies compete per heat. We'll refer to these babies by number rather than by name to protect the innocent, as well as the guilty.

By the end of this race the sharpest knife in your kitchen isn't going to be enough to cut through the tension in the room. So we're going to do you one little favor here at the beginning. Teaser alert: Baby #4 never crosses the starting line and is subsequently a total non-factor. Baby #3 streaks out at a record pace, gets within inches of the finish line, comes to a complete halt, and turns 90 degrees facing sideways toward lanes #1 and #2.

CHANGE OF MOMENTUM ~ Despite the repeated requests of his mother, Baby #3 never turns forward. So if you're keeping score at home you can now eliminate Baby #3 as a possible winner. Babies #1 and #2 both start slowly, but they each become simultaneously motivated and begin full throttle sprints toward the finish line.

Let's refocus on Baby #3; the fact that he had this race locked and loaded in the back of his diaper is no longer a concern. Projectile obstacles loom on the horizon, and the onlookers can see it on his face. There is about to be the most memorable confluence of three paths in the history of Lithuanian baby racing.

SURF'S UP ~ As Babies #1 and #2 hurdle neck and neck towards the finish line, Baby #3 hurls chunks into lane #2. Just when the audience feels certain the instant replay booth will need to be called in to judge a photo finish, Baby #2 hits the vomit pool and body surfs on to victory! To quote the Beach Boys, "Catch a Wave and You're Sittin' on Top of the World." Or at least on top of Lithuania.

For the record let it be known that, for the first time ever in Lithuanian baby racing history, an "assist" was officially awarded to Baby #3 in the story above. In conclusion, please allow us to summarize our thoughts as follows. Just because someone is a baby does not mean that he or she should be denied the thrills of high stakes competition, and it appears no nation understands that notion better than Lithuania.

> *Took off from the gate with a rocket glide*
> *Mom said that I would rock the comet ride*
> *The race took a twist then*
> *But man was I pissed when*
> *I just won that race in a vomit slide*

Chapter 3
ANIMAL ACTS

FROGGYLAND

AMPHIBIOUS MUSEUM ~ One of the most bizarrely delightful tourist attractions in the world is the Froggyland Museum which can be found in Split, Croatia. This museum holds the answers to many questions we feel sure you have probably previously pondered. What would it look like if frogs ran a circus, went to school, or played tennis? How about if they were carpenters, painters, or photographers? You can find the answer to these quirky questions and many more at the Froggyland Museum.

This festival of frogs was the life work of taxidermist Ference Mere who completed his project in 1920. This diverse collection of stuffed frogs posed in everyday human situations consists of 507 preserved frogs arranged in 21 cases of dioramas. Risking a descent into the depths of "too much information", allow us to describe Mere's methodology.

As a total perfectionist, Mere's technique was to never make any external incisions upon his frogs. So extrapolating this to his process, all of the frogs' innards were extracted through their mouths. Mere then stuffed each body with cork, also through the mouth, and proceeded to meticulously arrange each frog in his desired position.

Equal attention was also given to his props, down to the most minute detail. One frog in the classroom scene is raising two fingers to convey he knows the answer. The frog painter is holding a tiny brush as he approaches his easel and there is a tiny camera in the hand of the frog photographer. The Froggyland Museum is truly worth an internet image search. We assure you the result is an absolutely ribbet-ing experience.

STRIKE OF THE COBRA EFFECT

UNINTENDED CONSEQUENCES ~ Next we will tackle a venomous topic known as the Cobra Effect. The term stems from a specific event which we will describe here and it has come to be used in a general sense for other events which mirror the circumstances of the original Cobra Effect story. Here's our basic definition.

The Cobra Effect occurs when a seemingly logical solution to a problem ironically exacerbates the situation, resulting in the unintended consequence that the problem becomes even worse than it was before. Be honest; it's happened to all of us.

But next time it happens to you, perhaps you'll be comforted by the knowledge that the Smiths share your grief. And because of us, you can at least couch the embarrassment when explaining your faux pas to others by showing off the fact that you've mastered a cool sounding term applicable to the situation.

Here's what you do … utter the phrase "Damn Cobra Effect!" rather softly but loud enough so that others in the room will hear you. This will successfully shift the focus of attention from your mistake to the inevitable question, "What's the Cobra Effect?" Now you're armed, dangerous and ready to launch into your explanation. But first you'll need a little expertise, and that's what we're here for.

SNARING THE SNAKES ~ The original Cobra Effect story goes back to British India in the mid 1800's. Obviously spoiled by the virtually total absence of poisonous tropical snakes on the streets of London, the new British governor of India was totally appalled by the fact that on his afternoon stroll to the tea stand he would occasionally encounter live cobras on the streets of the capital of Delhi (It became New Delhi in 1927).

But those Brits are brainy and brilliantly bright. And the governor came up with a bold idea which may have foreshadowed why this whole colonialism thing was destined for failure from the get-go. The British governor issued a proclamation that a bounty would be paid for every cobra skin submitted by the Indian populace. Things started out well with industrious Indians setting traps everywhere to cage and capture countless cobras.

BEATING THE SYSTEM ~ However, in addition to those honest industrious Indians there were also some ingenious and illicitly inclined Indians. Seeing an obvious opportunity to bilk the Brits, an enterprising group of Indians began establishing, for lack of a better term, cobra farms. Cobras breed pretty well under any circumstances but when you ploy them with soft lights, fine wine and a snake charmer playing sultry jazz, you end up with enough snake eggs to freak out the Easter Bunny. The British were shoveling out a shitload of shillings.

Of course, there was an ironic and poetic justice about the whole thing. Some of the vast quantities of money the British were exploiting from the Indians, the Indians were retrieving from the British. Fair is fair, or perhaps a better way to put it would be unfair deserves unfair. And while we're rattling off clichés, inevitably in the Indian cobra scam, all good things must come to an end.

THE GIG IS UP ~ When the monthly bounty payout had quintupled from the inception of the program, the British came to the realization, that their rationalization that the Indians had just gotten really really good at their snake trapping skills was probably not the case. The Indians were cheating, so the snake bounty program was terminated with the British wishing there was some kind of market for used cobra skins and the Indian snake farmers looking to book vacations to the Mediterranean.

All of this is interesting, but there's a final and inevitable piece of the story you probably haven't anticipated yet. And it's this final piece that makes the British India story the defining moment in establishing it as the namesake for the concept known as the Cobra Effect. While the rural surrounding areas of Delhi had become increasingly infested with clandestine cobra farms to cash in on the British bounty, connect the dots and predict what happens when the bounty is discontinued.

THE PLAN BACKFIRES ~ Put yourself in the place of the snake farmers. You've got a farm full of poisonous snakes and nothing to do with them. It's not like there's a reptile animal shelter down the road where you can drop them off at the door. And while the best answer for humanity would be for you to kill the snakes, keep in mind that you admittedly are not one of the most ethical people in India in the first place.

Why spend your time and endanger your life in the process of killing poisonous animals when you have the option of doing nothing, letting the snakes go and just walking away from the whole mess? Ask yourself the following question… Which would you rather do: risk your life killing poisonous snakes or pack your bags for that aforementioned trip to the Mediterranean?

CONFIRMING THE COBRA EFFECT ~ So inevitably all the snakes were released and of course many of them found their way back to Delhi. Long story short, the British government spent 10,000 shillings to eradicate the cobras and ended up with twice as many as they started with. And that's the original story which generated the use of the term "Cobra Effect" for any situation where a seemingly logical attempt to solve a problem results in the unintended consequence of making the problem even worse than it was before.

REINDEER GAMES

TRANSGENDER REINDEER ~ Here's a storyline that came to us from a reader's suggestion. He had accessed this information in a publication from the Alaska Department of Fish and Game. According to that bureau, "While both male and female reindeer grow antlers in the summer each year, male reindeer lose their antlers at the beginning of winter, usually late November to mid-December. Female reindeer retain their antlers until after they give birth in the spring."

Obviously in the era of this new "Me Too" movement the analysis of gender relationships is totally front and center. And throughout the course of this book you will become well aware of the fact that we don't shy away from anything. But this holiday newsflash could not give us any choice other than to ponder the perceptions which have permeated our perspectives since prepubescent times. Long story short, all of Santa's reindeer have always had to be female.

TWISTED TV TALES ~ Do you remember the romantic holiday special where Rudolph the Red Nosed Reindeer met his soul mate? We do too. Okay let's do a show of hands here. How many of you knew that for that classic storyline to be true, Rudolph had to be transgender?

As we all collectively attempt to come to grips with the myths of our childhood, please allow us to throw out this one adult take on the recent realization of this rather rattling "reindeer revelation" rigmarole which might allow our entire audience to put this into proper perspective.

Here's the modernistic conclusion we've come to. Think about it. This should have been obvious from the beginning … does it not make sense that only a team of women would be able to drag a fat man in a red velvet suit all the way around the world in one night and not get lost?

THE BAT BOMB ~ A TRUE STORY FROM WWII

Assuming that North Korea hasn't done anything crazy since we wrote this book, the United States remains the only country in the world to have deployed nuclear weapons against human beings. The research to develop those weapons hit full stride in 1943 during WWII, and was known as the "Manhattan Project."

In our never-ending quest to seek out the unusual and share it with our readers, this piece is about another military project which was being explored simultaneously and had the parallel goal of bringing Japan to its knees and forcing surrender. It's a little bizarre and if we were sharing this with you on April Fool's Day you'd be sure we were pulling your leg. But it's all true and it might have brought about the same result, with a death toll coming in at a fraction of the 250,000 fatalities that occurred in Hiroshima and Nagasaki.

PROJECT INITIATED ~ The "Invasion by Bats Project" was actually initiated a few months before the Manhattan Project. It was originally conceived by a man named Lytle Adams who, as fate would have it, was a friend of First Lady Eleanor Roosevelt.

That connection afforded him an opportunity to present his idea to the U.S. military brass on January 12, 1942 and, as nocturnally flighty as the "bat bomb" idea seemed, the powers that be thought it was worth looking into and eventually spent the equivalent of 25 million dollars researching the subject.

From the get-go, do realize this is not a joke. So, now you're probably asking, "How's this gonna work?" Granted, we've got millions of bats in the U.S. and millions of enemies in Japan. But how do we use one to take down the other? The answer of course would be miniaturized time bombs clandestinely hidden in little bat satchels.

ANIMAL INSTINCTS - At this point we'll succumb to your will and provide the straightforward explanation. You're gonna love this. The first part of the plan was to capture a million bats which, at first, might seem to be a daunting task but turns out, this is the easy part.

Bats are very sound sleepers and if you enter one of their caves while they're upside down dreaming, you can pretty much just scrape them off the ceiling by the bagful. Just a warning here, if you're a bat lover, or a card-carrying PETA member, you're going to hate this story every inch of the way from here on out.

Once you've bagged your bats, the next step is to confuse their natural instincts and toss them all into a giant freezer. This induces hibernation and while bats hibernate every winter, this Christmas is going to be a little different. While visions of sugarplum insects dance in their tiny bat brains, this year Santa is not stuffing chocolate ants into their little stockings.

For the bats this probably foreshadows what kind of year this is going to be. Rather than a peaceful holiday bat-nap, this year a medical team is surgically attaching tiny bombs to their little bat bellies, not the most pleasant way to gain weight over the holidays.

At this point, all the military has to do is keep the bats chilled until time for deployment and the veterinary team subsequently hands over the cold critters to the hardware department. And if you think this story has been twisted and bizarre so far, rest assured, the devil's in the details of the deployment will devastate you.

HOW DOES THE BAT BOMB WORK? - Just to make sure and avoid any confusion, there are two concepts of the phrase "Bat Bomb" within the context of this segment. Each of the individual bats has had a tiny incendiary device (bomb) surgically sewn to its stomach.

But as we follow this process through to the end, the ultimate military goal is to end up with a huge metal cylinder, basically resembling a traditional bomb; only surprise, surprise, rather than being filled with a thousand pounds of TNT, each large bat bomb will be filled with a thousand hibernating mammals, each carrying its own mini bat bomb. Let the war games begin.

Continuing the theme of animal analogies, the question which remains the 800-pound gorilla in the room is, "How in the world could this concept be seriously considered as an alternative to the atomic bomb?" Well, next we're turning this piece over to *Mechanics Weekly*, for an explanation of how this bat bomb contraption would be successfully deployed. Obviously if you just drop a huge bomb full of bats out of a plane and allow it to fall directly to the ground the bats all die and you've accomplished nothing, except perhaps totally confusing the Japanese.

THE SPECIFICS ~ Now at this point you really need to focus. No matter how mechanically inclined you are, this process will rattle your brain. Here's how the dadgum thing is going to work. Inside each of the large bat bombs is a circular enclosure containing multiple layers with a thousand individual compartments, each holding one bomb-laden bat. U.S. war planes were to fly over Japan, drop the bat bombs shortly before daybreak, and wait for some precision timing to kick into effect.

During descent, a parachute initially deploys so the bat bombs float slowly to the ground. Next, the circular enclosures within the bomb are released. They expand in an accordion-like fashion exposing each of the 1,000 hibernating bats to the warm air and an escape route. As the parachutes descend slowly toward the Japanese earth, the warm air awakens the hibernating bats which instinctively fly away into the dark sky.

As if sewing tiny bombs to their bellies wasn't enough abuse, each of the bats has a thin thread running from its bomb to the circular enclosures. When the bat departs the enclosure, it breaks the thread which sets off a timed detonator essentially starting the clock counting down the last 30 minutes of the bat's life.

BATS DEPLOYED ~ What does the U.S. government have planned for these bats' final moments? Well, as you might suppose, no final meal requests will be honored. As dawn arrives and the first beauteous rays of sunshine begin to spill down upon the Japanese soil, the bats' nocturnal instincts kick in. To avoid the light, they seek shelter in the most accessible crevices, namely roofs, eaves, and attic spaces in the nearest buildings.

Not that we actively support the sacrifice of bats, but assuming PETA is unable to step in, at this point the incendiary devices attached to the bats begin to explode in rapid fire succession.

FIERY INFERNO ~ Strategically factor into this equation, the reality that most Japanese structures at this time are made of hardened paper, bamboo, and wood. Subsequently, they are extremely vulnerable to fire. This vulnerability is critical to the success of the attack plan.

Imagine the chaos that would have ensued if hundreds of thousands of Japanese structures started to pop on fire in rapid succession for no apparent reason. Follow up that scenario with a U.S. demand for Japanese surrender or the same thing will happen again.

JAPANESE SURRENDER ~ Knowing that it took two atomic bombs for the Japanese to surrender, there's no way they would have caved after just one bat bombing. But once the technology was in place the process could have been repeated every night in multiple locations. How many mornings could the Japanese have woken up with different cities totally ablaze before surrender was inevitable?

To this end, an entire simulated Japanese town was built at the Dugway Proving Ground in Utah. This was truly a make or break test because if it didn't work, there would not be the time or money to build another Japanese town.

Nervous scientists were up early on the morning of December 15, 1943 as the test bat bomb descended upon the simulated Japanese town. Within a half hour of daybreak "simulated Japan" was engulfed in flames; the bat bomb had been an overwhelming success.

IT WORKS! ~ The bottom line was that the military believed the bat bombs would actually work, test reports rating their efficiency at 10-30 times more effective than conventional bombs. The primary goal of incendiary bombs, at that point in history, was to start fires. If you are truly a numbers geek, the government report stated, "Regular bombs would produce probably 167 to 400 fires per bomb load, whereas bat bombs would produce 3,625 to 4,748 fires."

CHANGE OF PLANS ~ So why were the bat bombs never deployed? By the summer of 1944 it was determined that the tactic would not be combat ready until late 1945. At that point the decision was made that the goal for a quick end to the war would be better served by the use of the atomic bomb.

BAT FACTS ~ Meanwhile we'll close out this chapter by entertaining you with our favorite fun facts about bats. And keep in mind it isn't easy being a bat. Thanks to Dracula, a few cases of rabies, their pointy teeth, and the fact that they hang upside down to sleep, a lot of people are freaked out by bats. Turns out, you probably shouldn't be.

- Bats, which make up ¼ of the mammals on the planet, are the only mammals that can fly.
- A single brown bat can catch 1200 bugs in an hour.
- The average bat will probably outlive your dog; they can live up to 30 years.
- All bats see a little and some bats see very well.
- Bats are cleaner than you are, they spend two hours a day cleaning themselves and each other.
- Number of people in North America who have contracted rabies from bats in the past 50 years … under 10. If you are bitten by a bat, go to the doctor but no need to start funeral arrangements, you'll probably be just fine.
- Vampire bats don't suck blood, they lap it up. Stay calm. There are only three species of vampire bats in the world and none in the U.S. If you were to travel to Central or South America you might see a vampire bat bite a cow and then lick blood from the wound … no sucking involved.

Chapter 4
HISTORICAL HIJINKS

THE LEGEND OF PAUL REVERE

POETIC RIDE ~ Let us lead off this segment with two lines from an historical poem that everyone knows. Even if you hate poetry more than having a root canal done, we're sure you've heard the opening lines from the poem "Paul Revere's Ride" by Henry Wadsworth Longfellow.

> *Listen my children and you shall hear*
> *Of the midnight ride of Paul Revere.*

There is so much poppycock in the legend created by this poem that it's actually kind of fun to take the poem and pound the crap out of it with a history book, which is exactly what we're going to do here. Here's what Longfellow has wrong in his account of the iconic events which were initiated at the Old North Church in Boston that night of April 18, 1775.

LAMPOONING LONGSTANDING LEGENDS ~ We all remember the signal code detailing how the British were coming. It was, "One if by land, Two if by sea." In the poem, Paul Revere is described as being the recipient of the signal whereas in actuality, it was Revere's job to give the signal. The poem also implies that Revere rowed himself across the river, while in reality he was rowed by others.

The biggest fractured history component of this poem lies in the logistics. While it's true that someone did ride into Concord, Massachusetts on April 18, 1775, to warn that "the British are coming!", that person was **not** Paul Revere.

Paul Revere did visit Lexington, Massachusetts to provide an update on British troop movements at this time. But our Revolutionary War pal Paul never made it to Concord as stated in the poem.

TRUTH BE TOLD ~ Here's the actual historical background on this component. On April 18, 1775, Paul Revere, a silversmith; William Dawes, a cobbler; and Samuel Prescott, a doctor, join forces to embark upon a joint mission to bring the updated news on British advancements toward the city of Concord. Well, then as now, the best laid plans of mice and men sometimes go awry.

As the trio of Revere, Dawes and Prescott gallops toward Concord they are spotted by the British. Their mission compromised, they employ the trusted time-tested tactic of, "Let's split up so they don't catch all three of us." At this point Dawes heads back to Lexington, Prescott continues toward Concord, and Revere is captured and retained.

According to the Longfellow poem, on April 18, 1775 "It was two by the village clock when he (Revere) came to the bridge in Concord town." While the poetic flow is sweet, the historical accuracy sucks. The 2:00 am arrival occurred on April 19, and at that time Paul Revere's ass was in British custody. It was Doctor Samuel Prescott who was bringing the news of the British invasion to Concord.

SOMETIMES THE TRUTH HURTS ~ So now that our faithful readers have been freed from the shackles of the false premises characterized by the Paul Revere legacy, allow us to enlighten you with the rest of the truth. Do you want to know what was truly going on with Paul Revere later that night when he was immortalized by the Longfellow poem?

After having been captured by the British, his horse was taken from him and later Revere was set free. So in the moments when poetic history has Paul Revere patriotically riding into Concord, in actuality he wasn't gallantly galloping, he was woefully walking a lonely path back toward Lexington. Without a flashlight. Uber not an option.

All of which leaves us with the question of why Longfellow would write something that was so historically skewed? One would think that an intellectually astute writer such as Longfellow would have researched the specifics of this documented historical event to the extent that he would have been aware of the precise personnel involved.

PARTAKING IN POETRY ~ So as former teachers and current writers, here is the theory to which we are subscribing. Put yourself in the position of a poet . . . you are working on a piece that you feel may become magical. You've locked yourself into a catchy opening line of "listen my children and you shall hear" . . . Where are you going next?

Here are your two choices:

- Choice 1 ~ "Listen my children and you shall hear
      Of the midnight ride of Samuel Prescott"

- Choice 2 ~ "Listen my children and you shall hear
      Of the midnight ride of Paul Revere"

Bottom line, Paul Revere became legendary, under false pretenses, because his name happened to rhyme with the right word.

PARTISAN POETS ~ We'll pause at this point to passionately pick up our persuasive poetry pens. We were so incredibly inspired by the insanely infamous injustices in this Paul Revere legend that we decided to get off our high horse and write a song to right the wrong. Notice the poetry oozing out of us before we even get started.

Here is our history-correcting take on the situation from the perspective of Samuel Prescott, the man who actually did ride through Concord shouting out, "The British are coming."

Samuel Prescott's Ride

'Tis all quite well for kids to hear
"The Midnight Ride of Paul Revere"
But why should my name be forgot
As if Paul rode and I did not
I sallied forth, refused to fail
While Paul Revere, he was in jail
I warned the town and wrote this poem
While Paul Revere was walking home
*Why not **my** name? The reason's clear*
My name's Prescott and his Revere.

We hope you enjoyed our latest foray into the fine art of poetry. Next, we're going to continue our Revolutionary War theme by taking a trip to Bunker Hill. Grab your musket and come along.

BUNKER HILL BROUHAHA

BARROOM BANTER ~ One recent night we had walked across the street to our town tavern and were approached by one of our local readers who recognized us from seeing us in the paper. He said, "I've got an idea for you guys to write about which combines your holiday themes with correcting history." He went on to ask, "When you hear 'the Battle of Bunker Hill' mentioned, what first comes to mind?"

We'll ask you the same question right now and throw down the gauntlet challenging you to provide the answer to this without assistance from Google. Given the same challenge, the Smith brain trust briefly huddled at the bar and came up with the following response which was, "Bunker Hill was a Revolutionary War battle in which the colonists kicked some British ass."

Upon hearing our answer, we saw the eyes of our new-found friend light up and he said, "This is just what I was hoping to hear. Here's the setup for your 4th of July article where you set the record straight. Think of what you just said in your previous sentence and I'm here to inform you that you've got two things totally wrong. The British actually won the battle and it was not even fought at Bunker Hill."

FACT CHECK ~ While receiving a basic explanation at the bar that night, we made a mutual agreement to double check the facts of this story when we got home. Well, color us educated. Our informant was right on both counts, and here's the validation of the backstory.

Rewinding to the Revolutionary War, and regarding the location of this battle, the Colonial Army diverted from their original orders to take up positions on Bunker Hill and shifted to Breed's Hill, the next hill over. So, the Battle of Bunker Hill was actually fought on Breed's Hill.

Secondly, in our analysis of history, the British did win the battle sending the surviving colonists scampering, but there was a moral victory won by the Colonial Army. Despite their eventual retreat, the battle was a significant morale-builder for the inexperienced Americans. The casualty count read as follows . . . colonists: 100 killed, 300 wounded; British: 200 killed, 800 wounded.

The battle convinced the American colonists that patriotic dedication could overcome superior British military might. Additionally, the high price of victory at the Battle of Bunker Hill made the British realize that the war with the colonies would be long, tough and costly.

So there's our history lesson on the Battle of Bunker Hill. Your takeaway is that while it did serve as a moral victory to the American colonists, the British won the battle which was **not** fought on Bunker Hill.

LIGHTING UP THOMAS EDISON

LIGHT GOES ON ~ Once again the Smiths are here to straighten out some suspect history and cast a little light on what seems to us to be an historical injustice. Speaking of light, you could stop any fourth grader on the street, ask that ten-year-old who invented the light bulb, and the student would confidently respond, "Thomas Edison." Well … not so fast.

Thomas Edison applied for his patent on the light bulb in 1879, but there were a few predecessors. The truly illuminated know that the first light bulb was actually invented in 1802 by an Englishman named Sir Humphry Davy who created his light bulb by running an electric current through a platinum wire. Perhaps because it wasn't very bright or useful, Davy never even applied for a patent.

MODERN DAY BULB ~ In 1845, an American named J.W. Starr developed an incandescent light bulb that used a vacuum bulb and a carbon filament which was designed very similarly to Edison's. When Starr died, an Englishman named Joseph Swan continued his work. But the main problem with all light bulbs to this point was that the filament didn't burn long enough to make the bulb practical for any real-life use.

In 1877, Thomas Edison, with a full posse of assistants, started searching for a filament that would remain illuminated for a longer period of time. In 1879 the Edison team discovered that a carbonized cotton thread was the material they were looking for and applied for a patent on November 4, 1879.

So, Edison **did** invent the first light bulb that could last for a long period of time? Not really. Remember Joseph Swan from above? On February 3, 1879, Swan demonstrated a working light bulb in front of seven hundred people in a lecture theater in London, England. Guess what type of filament he used? Yep, carbonized cotton thread.

THINGS GET MESSY - From this point on, things got rather messy. There were patents in play on both sides of the Atlantic. There were lawsuits and counter lawsuits, which were won by Swan. It was at this point that the light bulb went off over Edison's head, figuratively speaking.

He invited Swan to form a company with him, which became known as Ediswan, and then Edison, using his superior resources, eventually bought Swan out. In the murkiness surrounding multiple lawsuits and transatlantic patent overlaps, history tends to defer to Edison as the inventor of the incandescent light bulb. Reality, however, seems to differ with history's tendency.

FINDING FERDINAND IN THE PHILIPPINES

SWITCHING SUBJECTS - In our maniacal meandering mission to unmuddy the mythically murky waters of history, we are going to sail out next on a misrepresented Magellan mission. In your high school history armada of memories, the next ship we sink will be that of Ferdinand Magellan.

After Christopher Columbus thought he had found India in 1492, the next magical historical milestone we were taught was that Ferdinand Magellan, a Portuguese captain in the service of Spain, became the first man to sail around the world (or circumnavigate the globe, for all you intellectuals out there).

PLAY BALL! - Let's set this thing up like a baseball game. The King of Spain, Charles V, has just thrown out the first pitch and it's the top of the first inning. Magellan is sent to the mound to begin the game.

Well, here's another haywire history alert. Magellan did not actually make it around the globe. We'll share the backstory. Let's set the Wayback Machine for August 10, 1519. Magellan sets sail from Seville, Spain with five ships and a crew of 250 men, but this voyage is not to be characterized by smooth sailing.

The three-year journey is plagued by terrible weather, maps that aren't up to date, starvation, and a violent mutiny. Let the games begin. Here are the details.

MIDDLE INNINGS - After departing in 1519, Magellan does make it all the way to the Philippines. Continuing our hypothetical baseball game, it would be roughly the equivalent of a pitcher making it into the 5th inning. Unfortunately for Magellan, his fate will be much more disheartening than getting yanked by the manager and sent to the showers.

Upon his arrival in the Philippines, an unsuccessful attempt to negotiate with the natives does not end well for our friend Ferdinand. You know those feisty Filipinos. A "complete game" is not destined to be on Magellan's stat sheet for this outing.

NO COMPLETE GAME - And while the Filipinos have certainly never thrown a baseball at this point, they are apparently quite adept at the javelin toss. Ferdinand Magellan's life ends with him resembling a human pin cushion, dead, face down on the beach with a dozen Filipino spears embedded in his back.

Not that it's the Smiths' goal to provide the buzzkill for every historical legacy which you've held dear since childhood, but here are the facts on this one . . . Of the five ships and 250 sailors that depart on Magellan's journey, only one ship returns home, there are only eighteen people on board, and Magellan is not one of them. So, allow us to add to our list of the historical poppycock we were taught in school; Magellan was not the first person to sail around the world.

In reality, that historical mantra is based upon the fact that Magellan's fleet, sponsored by Spain, did successfully have one of its original five ships limp home returning to port at Seville. Finalizing our thread of baseball references we'll summarize it as follows... While history ended up crediting Magellan with the win, he did not pitch a complete game.

TIPP HILL TALLY HO

ONE AND ONLY ~ For Halloween of 2018 we went to see an Alice Cooper concert in Syracuse. While we were there, we took the time to visit a landmark which can only be seen at one location in the United States. On top of Tipperary Hill in Syracuse, at the intersection of Milton Avenue and Tompkins Street, hangs the only upside-down stop light in America.

What do we mean by upside down? It's not something you've probably given much thought to, but the next time you see a traffic light you won't be able to get it out of your head because of this segment. The colors on a traffic light are, in descending order... red, yellow, green.

On Tipp Hill, as the locals refer to it, there is a traffic light that has the green on the top and the red on the bottom. It's been that way since 1925 and the reason behind it is a patriotic one. Patriotic, but not USA patriotic.

IRISH INSURGENCY ~ When the Erie Canal was built between 1817 and 1825, many workers on the project were Irish immigrants. When the project was completed these workers, who had been transient during the canal construction, needed to find permanent residences. Having become familiar with the area during their canal work, a large Irish population settled around Tipp Hill. The name of the hill was actually derived from the county of Tipperary, Ireland, from where the majority of the Syracuse Irishmen originally hailed.

So, the Irish community had been ensconced in the Tipp Hill section of Syracuse for a century when the advent of the automobile led to the installation of the first traffic light in 1925. Subsequently, the Irish youth took offense to the British red sitting on top of the Irish green and the red lens became a target, literally as well as figuratively.

Perhaps they were taking the imagined symbolism too far, but stones were repeatedly thrown, or launched with slingshots, breaking the red lights, over and over again. Supposedly, evil leprechauns throwing "Irish confetti" were even blamed for some of the mischief. Leprechaun logic notwithstanding, the city council eventually decided to relent to the Irish community. Little did they know that decades later their acquiescence would evolve into a tantalizing tourist attraction.

GREEN LIGHT GUESTS ~ Over the years Tipperary Hill has had some famous visitors; we'll share two quick examples. In 1966, in the beginning of his run for the presidency, Robert F. Kennedy came to Syracuse to deliver a speech. Where did he set up his podium? Under the upside-down traffic light. And to enhance the impact, the city programmed the traffic light to stay green for Kennedy's entire speech.

In 2005 Irish Prime Minister Bertie Ahern visited the United States. One of his stops was in Syracuse and he visited the Tipperary Hill Heritage Memorial, becoming the first foreign dignitary to do so. Yep, there's even an official memorial site at Tipp Hill and it actually has the distinction of being Syracuse's newest city park.

MONUMENTAL MOVEMENT ~ In 1997 local residents and business owners of Irish descent began a fundraising drive and garnered the support of the city to raze an old commercial building on the northeast corner of Milton and Tompkins to build a small park and erect the Tipperary Hill Heritage Memorial, the most outstanding feature of which is the Stone Throwers Monument.

In the corner of the park which is closest to the light, there is a life size bronze statue of a 1930 Irish immigrant family erected upon a marble base. The statue depicts the father pointing out the traffic light to his wife, with their daughter and son beside them, also gazing upward. Protruding from the back pocket of the son is a slingshot, perhaps subtly conveying the means by which the "Stone Throwers" were able to so accurately target their intended electronic victim.

LOCAL LORE ~ While we were in the area, we decided to visit Coleman's Authentic Irish Pub because we knew the previous owner Peter Coleman, now deceased, played a significant role in the fundraising effort to create the memorial park. Of the many bars we've visited, this stop turned out to be one of our most memorable. Upon the realization that we were working on a story about Tipp Hill for a paper in Rochester, the bartender was eager to share.

Nowadays people in the community openly discuss the names and ages of the original Stone Thrower's gang. This Irish mob ranged in age from 11-17 in 1925. And, according to the storyline we were provided, those names were kept very secretively in the community's archives prior to the establishment of the park. We asked why the park made it easier for the Irish community to share secrets that had been possessively protected for decades.

The answer we received was interesting and made sense. Having the only green-over-red traffic light in the world had always been a source of pride for the Irish community in Syracuse. And since they had the only traffic light that violated the official traffic laws of the nation, there was always a dormant fear that someday some stodgy tightass city official would come to power and make it a goal to go by the books and revert the traffic light to its original orientation.

DONE DEAL ~ But, once the memorial and statue became a permanent fixture in the city, the urban legend was so entrenched that the Irish community felt assured it could never be undone. And that's the story of the Tipperary Hill Heritage Memorial.

Irish blood runs thick in Syracuse. Keep in mind this is a city that hosts a St. Patrick's Day parade in February to kick off the Irish holiday season. The event is known as Green Beer Sunday and it falls on the last Sunday in February. Revelers dress in green, assemble at various pubs, and celebrate the arrival of the first green beer of the year. After quaffing a few, the celebrants pour into the streets and join together in a parade which marches, you guessed it, under the upside-down traffic light on Tipp Hill.

SEVENTY-FIVE FAMOUS MASONS

We did a piece about the murder of Captain William Morgan who was killed by the Masons in 1826 for revealing some of the secret society's secrets. That one backfired on the fraternal organization as a wave of anti-Masonic sentiment swept the country. It's an interesting story, but not one we chose to include in this book because, in all honesty, it's kind of a downer.

Our Masonic research however did inspire us to wax poetic on a dandy little bit of rhyme and verse which we've entitled "The Masons' Honor Roll Call." After consulting multiple lists of famous Masons, we compiled a roster of those we thought worthy of inclusion in our Hall of Fame roll call. We avoided fixation on the total number, but did think it would be cool if we came up with something round like 50 or 100.

As it turned out, our initial recruiting rally resulted in exactly 75 names, which we thought was round enough. So here's our premise. If you could somehow combine Heaven and Earth for what would be the most secret meeting ever, and get all these dudes in one room, we'll provide the roll call to make sure the gang's all here.

The poem is followed by an alphabetical listing of all the Masons mentioned in the poll along with a capsule biography to firm up the identity of each member. If you're a Mason and you hear your name called, please stand up.

So, here's "The Masons' Honor Roll Call." The following verses include a brief shout out to the most famous Masons in history. In no particular order here is your Masons' Hall of Fame. Let the roll call begin...

THE MASONS' HONOR ROLL CALL

The Washingtons, they were key
We had George and Booker T.

Colonel Sanders sure could cook
Kipling wrote *The Jungle Book*

Comedy had Richard Pryor
Lindbergh he kept flying higher

James Garfield had his politics
Houdini did his magic tricks

The Marquis de Lafayette
Benedict Arnold, we regret

Andrew Jackson was so manly
Livingstone, we presume, (but not Stanley)

William McKinley, he got shot
Gerald Ford almost, but not

Midnight Ride by Paul Revere
Jonathon Swift, Gulliver here

Judge Earl Warren shall adjourn
General MacArthur shall return

Cy Young's arm was one true cannon
15th Prez was James Buchanan

Mel Blanc, man of a thousand voices
Bugs and Daffy, favorite choices

Lewis & Clark did sally forth,
Blazed their way out west and north

Worked so hard, he rarely clocked in
James Monroe did write a Doctrine

Scottie Pippen's moves were cruel
Aaron Burr, he won the duel

John J. Astor, big wheel
Hoops legend, Shaq O'Neal

Adam Sandler, tell a joke
11th Prez was James K. Polk

Roy Acuff he wore cowboy boots
Alex Haley he wrote *Roots*

Clark Gable, he stayed calm
Truman dropped atomic bomb

Thurgood Marshall, thank the Lord
Walter Chrysler, Henry Ford

J. Edgar Hoover, always ready
Roosevelts, Frank & Teddy

Musicians always having fun
Mozart and Duke Ellington

Charles Mayo built a clinic
Andrew Johnson, total cynic

Charles Hilton, he had money
That Don Rickles, he was funny

Richard Byrd found the North Pole
After that came Nat King Cole

Sam Houston and Jim Bowie
Texans both, yip yip yahooey

Count Basie had some hits
Winston Churchill led the Brits

Joe Frazier, he was black son
So, of course, was Jessie Jackson

Glenn Ford, quite a fellow
Abbott was, (but not Costello)

King George the 4th, Steve Wozniak
Franklin says he wants his kite back

Founding Father was John Hancock
Conan Doyle, he wrote Sherlock

At quarterback we got John Elway
Dempsey boxed and Sugar Ray

Buzz Aldrin in his rocket
Kit Carson, Davy Crockett

King Edward VII, Mark Twain
King William IV, John Wayne

Michael Richards, Seinfeld's vent
William Taft was President

Oscar Wilde, he was gay
Hawaiian King Kalakaua

And of course, there's several others,
Add all seven Ringling Brothers.

Before we provide you with a "Who's Who" list of brief bios of the 75 most famous Masons, please allow us to share a conceptual overview of the backgrounds of our Super 75. The numbers breakdown in the following categories.

- Presidents: 14
- Blacks: 12
- Entertainers: 10
- Declaration of Independence signers: 9
- Sports: 7
- Royalty: 6
- Writers: 6
- Musicians: 5
- Businessmen: 5
- Explorers: 4

Of our 75 most famous Masons, the 8 who were still alive in 2020 were astronaut Buzz Aldrin, the Reverend Jessie Jackson, boxer Sugar Ray Leonard, basketball players Shaquille O'Neal and Scottie Pippin, actor/comedians Michael Richards and Adam Sandler and Apple's Steve Wozniak.

Here's our complete roster in alphabetical order including a brief bio for each man.

Bud Abbott ~ Comedian, Costello's partner
Roy Acuff ~ "King of Country Music" singer
Buzz Aldrin ~ Astronaut, made 3 space walks
Benedict Arnold ~ American General, traitor
John Jacob Astor ~ American businessman
Count Bassie ~ American jazz musician
Mel Blanc ~ Animation's greatest voice artist
Jim Bowie ~ Frontiersman, died at Alamo
James Buchanan ~ 15th President of the U.S.
Aaron Burr ~ Lawyer, 3rd U.S. Vice President
Richard Byrd ~ Admiral, North Pole explorer
Kit Carson ~ Frontiersman, U.S. Army officer
Walter Chrysler ~ Automobile manufacturer
Winston Churchill ~ British Prime Minister
Nat King Cole ~ American jazz pianist, singer
Davy Crockett ~ "King of the Wild Frontier"
Jack Dempsey ~ Professional boxer 1914-27
Arthur Conan Doyle ~ Sherlock Holmes writer
King Edward VII ~ British King from 1901-10
Duke Ellington ~ Jazz musician & composer
John Elway ~ Denver Broncos quarterback
Glenn Ford ~ Canadian-American actor
Gerald Ford ~ 38th President of United States
Henry Ford ~ U.S. automobile manufacturer
Joe Frazier ~ Heavyweight champion boxer
Clark Gable ~ Actor, "King of Hollywood"
James J. Garfield ~ 20th President of U.S.
King George IV ~ British King from 1811-20
Ben Franklin ~ Founding Father, statesman
Alex Haley ~ American author, wrote *Roots*
John Hancock ~ U.S. merchant, statesman
Charles Hilton ~ Hotel tycoon, businessman

J. Edgar Hoover ~ First Director of the F.B.I.
Harry Houdini ~ Escape artist and illusionist
Sam Houston ~ American soldier, politician
Andrew Jackson ~ The 7th President of U.S.
Jessie Jackson ~ U.S. civil rights activist
Andrew Johnson ~ The 17th President of U.S.
King Kalakaua ~ The last King of Hawaii
Rudyard Kipling ~ Indian-born British author
Marquis de Lafayette ~ French Statesman
Sugar Ray Leonard ~ U.S. professional boxer
Lewis & Clark ~ 1800's American explorers
Charles Lindbergh ~ Aviator, military officer
David Livingston ~ Physician, missionary
Douglas MacArthur ~ Five-star U.S. General
Thurgood Marshall ~ Supreme Court Justice
Charles Mayo ~ Co-founder of Mayo Clinic
William McKinley ~ 25th President of U.S.
James Monroe ~ The 5th President of U.S.
Wolfgang Mozart ~ Classical composer
Shaquille O'Neill ~ NBA basketball player
Scottie Pippin ~ NBA basketball player
James J. Polk ~ The 11th President of U.S.
Richard Pryor ~ Stand-up comedian, actor
Paul Revere ~ American patriot, silversmith
Michael Richards ~ Kramer in TV's *Seinfeld*
Ringling Brothers ~ First Family of the Circus
Don Rickles ~ Stand-up comedian, actor
Franklin Roosevelt ~ 32nd President of U.S.
Theodore Roosevelt ~ 26th President of U.S.
Colonel Sanders ~ Kentucky Fried Chicken
Adam Sandler ~ Actor, comedian, writer
Jonathan Swift ~ British writer, politician
William Taft ~ The 27th President of U.S.
Harry Truman ~ The 33rd President of U.S.
Mark Twain ~ American writer, humorist

Earl Warren ~ U.S. Supreme Court Justice
Booker T. Washington ~ Educator, author
George Washington ~ 1st President of U.S.
John Wayne ~ American actor, filmmaker
King William IV ~ British King from 1830-37
Oscar Wilde ~ Irish poet and playwright
Steve Wozniak ~ Inventor, Apple co-founder
Cy Young ~ Major League Baseball pitcher

CHAPTER 5
TOP 10 COUNTRY STORIES

In case you hadn't noticed, the world is a funny place. As a matter of fact, we actually found the planet so comical we wrote a book about it a few years ago. It featured a blurb we wrote about every country and territory in the world, past and present, which included all the basic facts along with our irreverent take on whatever it was that made each particular country a little bit quirky or vulnerable. Then we put together our Top 10 List of the Greatest Geography Stories in History. That's what we're about to share with you here.

Our attitude in writing this book has been to provide you fine folks with nothing but the best and don't worry, we're not about to start letting you down now. Several of the entries in our list are micronations, which is a term we probably need to explain. We'll offer two versions. In layman's terms it's when you make up your own country and have fun pretending you're the real deal. We are the micronation of Ganonda-Gonyea-Smitty-2-ville and we have the flag flying out front to prove it. For a more formal version, we'll offer below the official glossy entry from our book:

A micronation is an entity that claims to be an independent nation or state but is not officially recognized by world governments or major international organizations. Micronations are distinguished from other entities by expressing a formal and persistent, even if unrecognized, claim of sovereignty over some physical territory. Several micronations have issued coins, flags, postage stamps, passports, medals, and other items, which are rarely accepted outside of their own community. A primary goal of a micronation is to get any sovereign government to officially respond to the micronation, or a situation created by the micronation, in order to elevate the micronation's status and credibility.

TOP 10 COUNTRY STORIES PREVIEW

10 - ROSE ISLAND - After American sitcom's radical ridicule, Italian military gets cantankerously cranky and blusterously blows up micronation in the Adriatic Sea.

9 - SAN MARINO - The world's oldest republic is formally founded by a pioneering pack-it-up priest who infiltrates Italy, looking for a spaciously serene and sacred site.

8 - MOOSYLVANIA - Imagine Minnesota might serve as the humorous home for the bodacious Bullwinkle J. Moose to substantiate his sweet summer soiree setting.

7 - SEALAND - Thrillingly thriving for decades on auspiciously abandoned British WWII military platform in the North Sea, Sealand pedals pirate radio and provocation.

6 - PITCAIRN ISLAND - Mutiny on the Bounty survivors playfully propagate with tantalizing Tahitian treats, inundate island with infants & emergency evacuation ensues.

5 - ALCATRAZ - Naughty Native Americans daringly declare independence, access abandoned prison, & eagerly engage ceremonious celebrity support. Frolicking fun until nixed by Nixon.

4 - MICRONESIA - The quirky country that was perpetually passed around like a fearfully fated fruitcake fulfilling its calamitous curse like a dreadfully deadly disease.

3 - CHRISTIANIA - Hallowed haven for progressive thought and creativity, or harrowing harbor full of sketchy squalid squatters and dangerous drug dealers?

2 - COCOS (KEELING) ISLANDS - The coincidental coalescing of one family's virtuous values with another's horny harem; what could possibly go wrong?

1 - CLIPPERTON ISLAND - This bizarrely trepidatious tale of rape & murder definitely demonstrates that sometimes it's good to be the last man standing & sometimes it's not.

10 ~ ROSE ISLAND ~ The Republic of Rose Island was a short-lived micronation on a 4,300-square-foot man-made platform in the Adriatic Sea, seven miles off the coast of Italy. It was constructed in 1967, supported by nine pylons, and furnished with a number of commercial establishments, including a restaurant, bar, nightclub, souvenir shop, post office and radio station. Here's what happens next.

The platform declares independence from Italy on June 24, 1968. Rose Island's actions eventually become viewed by the Italian government as a ploy to raise money from tourists while avoiding national taxation, and the Italian Navy subsequently lands on the island and takes it over in what the Rose Island government refers to as a "military occupation."

SITCOM SATIRE ~ Right now we are going to offer one of our more inspired examples of how life sometimes imitates art. The sitcom *That Girl* starring Marlo Thomas was a hit show in the late 1960's. Her father, Danny Thomas, was a major star in the early TV era, as well as being the founder of St. Jude's Children's Hospital. Marlo subsequently took on his role of spokesperson for that charitable organization.

Just prior to the Italian takeover of Rose Island *That Girl* runs an episode where Marlo's character talks about a "game night" with her boyfriend. She says, "We played the board game *World Power* where each player gets to be a country. I was Italy. I surrendered three times in the first half hour."

LET'S WIN ONE ~ Possibly embarrassed by the fact that they are media-mocked by Marlo, the Italian army seems motivated to identify a victim they can vanquish. So let's think this over. You're Italy and still reeling a bit from that WWII setback. Hypothetically, you're looking for the most winnable war possible. Doesn't Rose Island have "can't miss" written all over it?

On February 10, 1969, the Italian Army storms the platform and oversees the evacuation of all people from Rose Island. In an apparent effort to involve as much of its military as possible, the Italian Navy is called in next. On February 13, 1969 they use explosives to destroy the platform, an act later portrayed on postage stamps issued by Rose Island's self-declared government in exile.

9 ~ SAN MARINO ~ Since we're in Italy anyway how 'bout we take a trip inland and swing by San Marino which boasts a few interesting storylines. Totally surrounded by Italy, it is one of only three sovereign enclave nations in the world. As implied by the beginning of that previous sentence, an enclave is a country completely surrounded by a single other country. The other two are the Vatican City (Italy) and Lesotho (South Africa).

SORENITY SOUGHT ~ Here's the country's backstory … Saint Marinus, the man after whom the country is named, is born in modern-day Croatia before crossing the Adriatic Sea to become a pastor in Rimini in modern-day Italy. Upon persecution there, he moves further inland, sets up new digs, starts a small church on September 3, 301 AD, and proclaims the surrounding area "The Most Serene Republic of San Marino."

Seems crazy, but what the hell it worked, and serenity notwithstanding, more than 1700 years later San Marino lives on as the oldest surviving sovereign state and constitutional republic in the world. Favorite San Marino "fun fact" … it is the only country in the world with more vehicles than people.

8 ~ MOOSYLVANIA ~ Moosylvania is an island micronation, located in the Lake of the Woods along the Canada – United States border, that served as a plot device created by Jay Ward for his *Rocky and Bullwinkle* TV show. Ward was notoriously known for his outrageous, over-the-top public relations antics and the impressive degree to which he executes his crusade on this project we'll describe below.

Moosylvania has no permanent population, and the only temporary resident is cartoon character Bullwinkle J. Moose, the island's namesake and governor, and the backstory of the micronation is generally established through his lines in that show. Conditions are said to be harsh and unpleasant which Bullwinkle turns into a plus. He only stays two weeks at a time because, "After two weeks here, anyplace else feels like Heaven."

Moosylvania is in a state of terra nullius since neither Canada nor the United States wants to claim the land, and each country says it belongs to the other. The American portion of the Lake of the Woods is in the state of Minnesota and in one geographical quirk there is actually a chunk of Minnesota that you can only get to by crossing the lake or going through Canada.

NATIONAL CAMPAIGN ~ In the fall of 1962 Jay Ward, creator and producer of the *Rocky and Bullwinkle* show, decides to initiate a campaign for statehood for Moosylvania. He conducts a west-to-east cross-country tour in a decorated van, gathering signatures on a petition supporting Moosylvania statehood. In terms of publicity stunts it is an absolute stroke of genius, with much of the country joyfully playing along with the ploy.

After arriving in Washington, his entourage seeks an audience with President Kennedy. However, as fate would have it, their arrival at the White House happens to coincide with the Cuban Missile Crisis and the Moosylvania entourage is quickly escorted off the White House grounds. Damn Cubans ruin everything. After the statehood effort fails, Ward declares the Republic of Moosylvania to be a micronation which was ultimately his goal all along.

7 ~ PITCAIRN ISLANDS ~ Now let's leave the Lake of the Woods behind and head for the South Pacific. A possession of the U.K., the Pitcairn Islands are a group of four volcanic islands which was first discovered by the Portuguese in 1606. Its subsequent history has a few strange twists that firmly entrench it in our "Best Stories" list.

TWIST #1: The islands are inhabited by the descendants of the survivors of the actual historical event of the mutiny on the Bounty, along with the Tahitians who were accompanying them. Here's how this story goes down. In 1790, nine of the mutineers from the Bounty, along with the native Tahitian men and women who are with them (six men, eleven women and a baby girl), settle on Pitcairn Island and set fire to the Bounty.

The wreck is still visible underwater in Bounty Bay, discovered in 1957 by *National Geographic*. Despite British attempts to locate the

Bounty survivors after the 1790 disappearance, there is no human contact until a U.S. ship happens upon the settlement in 1808. Information is passed on to the British who finally show up in 1814 to figure out what the hell happened. At this point all the survivors of the original incident are pardoned and Pitcairn is claimed as a U.K. territory in 1838.

TWIST #2: By the mid-1850s, the Pitcairn community is outgrowing the island and its leaders appeal to the British government for assistance. They are offered Norfolk Island which, although it is almost 4,000 miles away, was uninhabited and habitable. In May 1856, the entire Pitcairn community of 193 people sets sail for Norfolk arriving in June after a miserable 3,943-mile five-week trip. But after eighteen months on Norfolk, half of the Pitcairn Islanders decide to return to their home island; five years later the other half follow. So, bottom line, they all left and they all came back. The current Pitcairn population is 50.

6 ~ SEALAND ~ From the South Pacific let's head to the North Sea off the coast of England where we find Sealand, a self-declared micronation. It begins as a British offshore anti-aircraft platform during WWII, serving to fend off German mine-laying planes. During the war, the platform housed 107 U.K. sailors on its 658-square-yard deck which is 7.5 miles off the coast.

In 1967 Pirate Radio broadcaster Paddy Roy Bates occupies the platform and sets it up as a base for his pirate station "Radio Essex." A year later Bates' son fires a rifle at a British work crew that is repairing an automated buoy near the platform, and is arrested for firearms violations since Bates and his family are still considered British citizens. Bates is acquitted, due to the platform being three miles outside of the U.K.'s oceanic claim, located in international waters.

Seeing an opportunity, Bates declares the platform to be the "Principality of Sealand" giving his tiny nation the motto E Mare Libertas (From the Sea, Freedom), writes a national anthem, and starts issuing stamps and currency. He states that the court ruling gives him the right to declare the open-sea platform as a sovereign nation. The

Bates family continues to occupy the platform and look for opportunities to bolster their claim of sovereignty.

FOREIGN INVASION ~ The most significant event in this regard occurs in 1978 when a party of German and Dutch adversaries attempt a violent takeover of Sealand. The attempt fails and the perpetrators are captured. Although the attack is certainly not supported on any level by the governments of Germany or the Netherlands, those two countries are put in the position of having to send government officials to Sealand to negotiate the release of their citizens.

Official dealings with established sovereign nations is the ultimate micronation dream, and having the U.K., Germany and the Netherlands on its resumé puts Sealand at or near the top of the micronation world.

5 ~ **ALCATRAZ** ~ Definitely one of the most interesting stories in the loop. Here's the scoop. The Native American Occupation of Alcatraz Island lasts for nineteen months, from November 20, 1969, to June 11, 1971, before being forcibly ended by the U.S. government. The Occupation is predicated upon the fact that the 1868 Treaty of Fort Laramie between the U.S. and the Sioux Nation stipulated that should any former Sioux land surrendered to the U.S. become "retired, abandoned or out-of-use" that land would be returned.

The Sioux had previously inhabited Alcatraz, and since the penitentiary closed in 1963, and the island had been declared "surplus federal property" in 1964, activists feel Alcatraz qualifies for a reclamation. In the early morning hours of November 20, 1969, eighty Native Americans, including students, married couples and children, set out to occupy the island and establish an independent state. A Coast Guard blockade prevents most of them from landing, but fourteen protesters do make it to the island to begin the Occupation.

The initial landing party is joined by many more in the following days, including Joe Morris (head of the Longshoreman's Union, which threatens to close area ports if the occupiers are removed), and the man who would soon become the "Voice of Alcatraz", John Trudell. On Thanksgiving Day, hundreds of supporters make their way to Alcatraz to celebrate the Occupation. In December, Trudell begins making daily radio broadcasts from the island, and a daily newsletter follows in January.

FAMOUSLY FEATURING ~ Grace Thorpe, daughter of legendary Native American athlete Jim Thorpe, is one of the occupiers and helps convince celebrities including Jane Fonda, Anthony Quinn, Marlon Brando, Jonathan Winters, Buffy Sainte-Marie and Dick Gregory, to visit and show their support. John Fogerty's rock group Creedence Clearwater Revival supports the Occupation with a $15,000 donation that is used to buy a boat, named the Clearwater, which provides reliable transport to and from Alcatraz. At the height of the Occupation there are over 400 people living on the island.

As the Occupation becomes more and more of a thorn in the side of the Nixon administration, the government begins to look for ways to compromise the movement. To this end, the government is able to infiltrate the hierarchy of leadership at Alcatraz and instigate infighting among various factions. Once the momentum of the Occupation has been slowed, the government goes on to cut off all electrical power and telephone service.

Then a fire of disputed origin (government sabotage?) destroys numerous buildings on the island, further reducing moral. Finally, left without power, phones, fresh water, and in the face of diminishing public support and sympathy, the number of occupiers begins to dwindle. On June 11, 1971, a large force of government officers remove the remaining 15 people from the island, thus constituting the end of the trail.

4 ~ MICRONESIA ~ Let's move on from that national story to our favorite fruitcake of intriguing international tales, a tale characterized by a course of calculated curses. The traditional fruitcake storyline is that the recipient wants to unload it as soon as possible. In the strange storyline of Micronesia, the series of controlling countries that own the islands make the mistake of clinging to them until the curse kicks in.

We ask you now to faithfully follow the foibles of the Federated States of Micronesia, which is an independent sovereign island nation comprised of 607 islands in the Western Pacific. The story starts when

Spain claims the islands in the early 1800's but never inhabits them until 1887.

Thus begins what we refer to as the "Fruitcake Phase of the Federation." This is an historically quirky sequence where the islands apparently become cursed and every time a major country assumes control, it loses its next major war and subsequently has to surrender the islands, thereby passing on the curse. A total of four countries would be afflicted by this curse.

CURSE #1 ~ After losing the Spanish-American War to the U.S., Spain is compelled to sell the islands to Germany in 1899.

CURSE #2 ~ Germany of course loses WWI, after which the League of Nations makes Micronesia a Japanese Protectorate, thus passing on the curse and foreshadowing Japan's fate in WWII.

CURSE #3 ~ Japan, now the unwitting owner of the curse, is subsequently destined for disaster in WWII. After that defeat, Japan is stripped of all its international territories, including Micronesia. At that point, in 1946, the United Nations hands off Micronesia to the United States, thus passing on the curse to our country. If only we'd known!

CURSE #4 ~ Unfortunately our country is not astute enough to realize the curse that has been passed on to us. The U.S. hangs on to the islands of Micronesia too long and becomes engaged in the Vietnam War. After that defeat the greatest minds of our nation, finally recognizing the curse, grant independence to Micronesia in 1986.

The U.S. is currently sending out free "Micronesia Vacation" brochures to the leaders of Iran and Russia. Keep your fingers crossed.

3 ~ CHRISTIANIA ~ Within the city of Copenhagen, Denmark lies a micronation which is truly unlike any other place on Earth.

Christiania is an 84-acre enclave established in 1971 when a party of young artists, hippies, and squatters take over an abandoned military base on the edge of town and declare themselves to be the free nation of Christiania. What has ensued in the past 45 years has been a fascinating dance between the mother nation of Denmark and her micronation child of Christiania.

After taking over the former military barracks, the Christianites declare their new home turf to be a "free zone" beyond the reach of Danish law. One might think the Danish government would have just stepped right in and squelched the whole thing decades ago, but ironically Denmark and Christiania have developed a bit of a mutually symbiotic relationship.

Forty-five years later Christiania not only survives, it thrives as Denmark's second most popular tourist attraction and the largest and most enduring hippie commune in history, still rockin' on with 900 permanent residents and half a million guests a year. No other micronation has legitimate control of more truly valuable territory than Christiania.

Certainly, the most controversial aspect of Christiania has been the totally open use and sale of marijuana. The heart of the enclave is a main street which, since the inception of Christiania, has been lined with marijuana vendors. While marijuana is still officially illegal in Denmark, enforcement in general is lax, and enforcement in Christiania has traditionally been almost non-existent. The Danish government has obviously come to the conclusion that any negatives stemming from the casual use of marijuana are outweighed by the positives generated by this motivated, ecology-oriented, self-governing, racially diverse and extremely tolerant community.

We were able to obtain a couple of quotes from Tom Freston who visited Christiania both recently and in the beginning days. We feel his comments put a particularly apropos perspective on how Denmark's "social experiment" has stood the test of time. He said that when he first visited, "The free town seemed more a festival to me than a society. I could not imagine it lasting. People would flock there for a while, I knew, but criminal elements, motorcycle gangs, and party people, the usual potpourri of miscreants, would surely soon outnumber the idealists. The locusts would come, as they did in Haight-Ashbury. Inevitably, the government would forcibly close it down. Obviously, I didn't know the Danes."

Freston's modern-day perspective was that, "Christiania has grown up to be a cool, verdant little village in a corner of Copenhagen. I had underestimated the work ethic and the diligence of the Danes. They have built an entire settlement of spare, humble, Hobbit-like homes that surrounds a lake and runs along gravel paths and cobblestone roads that wind through woods to the seaside." Sounds quite picturesque, doesn't it?

Sure, there have been issues over the years, but at this point Christiania's permanent survival is a damn good bet. Denmark is proud of it now. Danish businesses and organizations use Christiania as a local showcase for their foreign friends and guests. After all, these are people who first stood up to the government, then stood up to criminal elements, then took in the poor and underprivileged, then built their own homes, were racially diverse, eco-friendly, and finally sent the world a message about the tolerance and creativity of Denmark.

Noted Danish entrepreneur, Jonas Hartz said, "It's impossible to imagine Copenhagen without Christiania. No Danish government could close it down. Thousands of people would immediately march in the streets for them." After all, grown-ups need playgrounds too.

2 ~ COCOS (KEELING) ISLANDS ~ Next let's make the always difficult transition from getting high in Denmark to getting laid in the Indian Ocean. For what it's worth, these two aforementioned activities should probably both be on your bucket list. Now we're going to ask you one of those haunting questions that you won't be able to get out of your mind for the rest of the day. If you only do one of these two activities, which one would you choose? And why?

Picture in your mind the world map you remember since grade school. Go to the Indian Ocean, and located about halfway between the southern tip of India and the western tip of Australia are the Cocos (Keeling) Islands.

Some quick background on these islands which are a territory of Australia … the whole shebang is comprised of 27 islands, only two of which are inhabited, and those only sparsely. The total population is only 544. One quirky fun fact is that the Cocos (Keeling) Islands is the only country or territory in the world to have a set of parentheses in its official title.

The dual name reflects the fact that islands have historically been known by both titles and when Australia took over in 1955 the decision was made to go with the parentheses. Beginning this story, the Cocos (Keeling) Islands are first sighted by British Captain William Keeling in 1609, hence that half of the name; the other half being derived from the fact that there are coconut trees all over the damn place.

ISLAND ARRIVALS ~ The islands remain uninhabited until the early 19th century when the first two almost simultaneous attempts to inhabit them result in an interesting conflict between two wealthy Englishmen. In 1825 Captain John Clunies-Ross stops at the islands on a trip to India, nails up a Union Jack, and makes plans to return and settle with his wife, kids and mother-in-law.

Meanwhile Alexander Hare who, although he had become rich as a politician in Malaysia, decides he "cannot confine himself to the tame life that civilization affords." He subsequently acquires a harem of 40 Malay women and moves the whole party to the islands. Sounds like a fun guy, right?

Frivolity ensues, but not for long. The Malaysian harem hoedown is not the healthy habitat Clunies-Ross had envisioned for his family and upon his return the pair of men clash immediately. The deciding factor in the conflict turns out to be that Clunies-Ross has also brought eight sailors with his family and the sailors "began at once the invasion of the new kingdom to take possession of it, women and all."

SEXCAPADES ~ After some time, Hare's harem begins deserting him, and finding themselves mates amongst Clunies-Ross' sailors. Disheartened, Hare leaves the island and returns to the mundane world of politics. It's always tough to leave a harem behind, but sometimes a man's gotta do what a man's gotta do.

So going back to the story of its earliest inhabitants, perhaps the greatest lesson to be learned from the saga of the Cocos (Keeling) Islands is that next time you plan to sail to a tropical island with your own personal harem, if upon your arrival you are unexpectedly greeted by numerous single sailors, keep your harem on your boat and keep on sailing.

1 ~ CLIPPERTON ISLAND ~ When the French discover this island in 1711 a rollicking rush of romanticism compels them to name it Passion Island. Things have pretty much gone downhill since then, but it makes for a hell of a story. You don't make #1 on a Smith Top 10 List without some passionate rollicking. We wouldn't have it any other way.

Flashing back to #3 and #2 in this countdown, we mentioned that getting high in Denmark and getting laid in the Indian Ocean should definitely be on your bucket list. Alleviating the fear that your list becomes too long, rest assured Clipperton Island is no place you'll want to visit soon.

But putting the silver lining on the Clipperton cloud, the good news would be that if you found yourself there today, you'd be a lot better off than you would have been 100 years ago. Here's the scoop. Just to establish the general location of where you would not want to be, Clipperton is a tiny island located 671 miles southwest of Mexico in the eastern Pacific Ocean.

If you were to go there today you would find basically a sandy desert, with several hundred palm trees. Throw in a few crabs and birds and you have your present-day Clipperton Island. Not a soul in sight and not a lot going on now, but about a century ago the place was hoppin'.

TRAIL OF GREED ~ After its 1711 discovery by the French, a bizarrely twisted path ensues. The island has been variously claimed by the following countries, in the following years, (for the following reasons): Mexico in 1848 (we're closest), the U.S. in 1856 (we want the mining rights), France in 1858 (we found it first), and the U.K. in 1906 (we just paid off the Mexicans).

In 1909 all the countries involved agree to let King Victor Emmanuel of Italy make an impartial decision on who should get the island. The

King goes right to work on the assignment and promptly renders his decision ... in 1931. In the meantime, all hell breaks loose. Read on.

By 1914 around 100 people—men, women, and children—are living there, resupplied every two months by a ship from Acapulco. With the escalation of fighting in the Mexican Revolution, the regular resupply visits cease and the inhabitants are left to their own devices.

LAST CHANCE BASH - In late 1915, the U.S.S. Lexington arrives and advises the now 75 remaining inhabitants that this is their "last chance" to be guaranteed safe transit back to the mainland. Twenty-five of the Clippertonians opt to go home for the holidays, leaving about 50 attendees at the Clipperton Island New Year's Eve bash welcoming in the year 1916. Unfortunately, the party will soon be over for most of the celebrants.

Disease, famine, and a disastrous attempt to sail after a passing ship for help all take their toll, and by mid-1917 the population is down to 17. Still alive are 2 men, 8 women, and 7 children. Then a mysterious accident at the lighthouse whittles the population down to 16 and leaves lighthouse keeper Victor Alvarez as the last man standing.

Alvarez promptly proclaims himself "Husband King" and begins a brief orgy of rape and murder, before being killed himself by Tirza Rendon, one of the cranky recipients of his unwanted affections. Not long after Álvarez's death, four women and seven children (the last survivors) are picked up by the U.S.S. Yorktown on July 18, 1917.

The Epilogue ... In 1931 the King of Italy declares Clipperton to be a French possession. The French do repair the lighthouse and establish a military base on the island, but that only lasts for seven years until 1938. Clipperton has been uninhabited ever since, although it was briefly used by the U.S. military during World War II.

Of all the quirky stories we have come across while writing our book about geography, this one settled in as #1 on our list of the strangest and most bizarre. When you can combine a four-way international dispute, rape, murder, disease, and famine all onto a small island your drama-per-square-mile ratio doesn't get much higher than this.

CHAPTER 6
CRIMES AND PASSION

LIZZIE BORDEN'S 40 WHACKS

We are going to start out this segment of our second book with a story of how we came to write the first one. As we had been writing the feature that filled the back page of our local paper for several years, our publisher Chris Carosa had been encouraging us to write a book. While we had found the concept enticing, we were going to need 50,000 words on a single topic and we had been enjoying our pattern of playfully flitting through pieces on various subjects including music, sports, travel, history and human interest.

In an endeavor that originally had no book plans whatsoever, we had written a one-week feature on the "cause célèbre" trials of Lizzie Borden and Charles Manson which we were just patiently sitting on. At the beginning of 2019, we became aware of a unique hat trick of 50th anniversaries looming on the horizon over the course of just a one-month period during that approaching summer. Yes, the sultry summer of '69 proved to be an eventful one.

Within a month-long period of time, crazy things begin to happen all over the solar system. On July 20, Neil Armstrong becomes the first man to walk on the moon; on August 8–9, the Manson Family commits the Tate-LaBianca murders in Los Angeles, California; and on August 15–18 the Woodstock Music Festival takes place in Bethel, New York, and it also happened to be the month we met.

So, this combined set of circumstances becomes a sign for us. We decide to pick one of these events and see if there's enough substance to warrant a major work on our part. While the Manson tale is totally tragic, the related nuances are truly intriguing. The trail of sex and drugs and rock and roll become the fodder for our first book which was called *The Beatles, The Bible & Manson: Reflecting Back with 50 Years of Perspective.*

In the meanwhile, we have been sitting on a half-week feature on Lizzie Borden that we are finally going to be able to share with everyone here. That's where we'll take you next, and following that we'll serve up a tasty sample from our first book.

IN JEOPARDY! ~ We're going to blame *Jeopardy!* for what is going to happen next. We were watching the show one evening and a question came up about Lizzie Borden. This intrigued us a bit because as we queried each other, we realized that neither one of us had a firm grasp on the details of that story. So we challenged ourselves to share everything we could remember off the top of our heads before heading to the internet.

Our Lizzie Borden brainstorm resulted in a recollection of three basic facts. The story involved axe murders, it happened a long time ago, and there was some kind of iconic poem written about it. Our research revealed the following nutshell summary. The long-story-short of it was that in 1892 Lizzie's parents were both victims of axe murders and Lizzie was the primary suspect.

Of course, if there weren't more to it than this we wouldn't suck you in for the whole story. But anywhere murder and mayhem manifest themselves, you know you can count on the Smiths to provide the sordid details. Let's seize the moment and start the soiree.

DETAILS REVEALED ~ During our direct assault on history, we uncovered some interesting details related to the Lizzie Borden story which began on August 4, 1892. Some of the sordid details proved positively fascinating, which adds to the notoriety of the Lizzie legend. The case is considered to be a forerunner of some of the "cause célèbre" trials that ensued in more modern times.

The definition of the French term "cause célèbre" is "a trial arousing widespread controversy and heated public debate." Examples spanning time would include from the early 1900's … Bruno Hauptmann (Lindberg baby); through the late 1900's … O.J. Simpson (murdered wife); to the 2000's … Amanda Knox (Italian roommate).

WICKED WHACKS ~ Returning to the Lizzie Borden story, another aspect that struck us is the degree to which our minds are shaped by movies, books and poems that are written more for entertainment than factual purposes. Take Lizzie Borden for example, and chant along with us the poem by which she was immortalized.

Lizzie Borden took an axe
And gave her mother forty whacks
When she saw what she had done
She gave her father forty-one

Great rhyme scheme, nice meter and very memorable lines. But some of the primary facts are way off. For the record, the father was killed first and he actually was whacked only 18 times, but of course "eighteen" doesn't rhyme with "done."

LIZZIE LIBERATED ~ The other problem with the poem is that if it is all you remember; you are going to be missing a most important fact. In the subsequent jury trial Lizzie was acquitted. Truth be told however, the trial had in common with the O.J. Simpson trial the fact that everybody pretty much knew the accused did it. But the defense managed to create just enough of a shadow of a doubt that the jury couldn't bring back a conviction.

So, what created the doubt in the Lizzie Borden case? There was no bloody glove, but there were multiple factors muddying the water. Despite the fact that there were numerous people around, nobody actually saw either murder.

To explain the "numerous people" mentioned above, in addition to the victims, also living in the house at the time of the murders were Lizzie, her sister, an uncle, and a maid. Throw in a couple estranged relatives residing in town and your suspect pool floweth over.

SHODDY POLICE WORK ~ Another problem was that the trial was plagued by some very shoddy police work, possibly perpetuated by the fact that Lizzie was a sweet-looking Christian girl whose lesbian tendencies were not revealed until decades after the trial. A possible motive floated later was that Lizzie had a falling out with her parents over her sexual orientation.

This theory certainly seems plausible. During the 1890's, the outing of Christian lesbians was not an event to be taken lightly. It's the type of exposure which could leave a girl feeling like she might have an axe to grind, so to speak.

Important evidence was not gathered from the house in the immediate aftermath of the murders. The murders occurred on August 4, and at the trial, one of Lizzie's friends testified that she had seen Lizzie burning a dress on August 8, similar to the one she was wearing on the day of the murders. Interestingly, the defense never challenged this claim.

VERDICT RENDERED ~ In addressing the jury before deliberation, the judge delivered a lengthy summary which seemed to support the defense. The jury followed his lead and acquitted Lizzie Borden in a deliberation that took just 90 minutes, subsequently making her an orphaned heiress rather than a convicted killer. Sometimes it's a short walk from the hangman's gallows to the hallowed gallery of exonerated murderers.

For good reason, the story has remained a topic in American pop culture ever since and has been depicted in various films and literary works. At this point, however, it's too late to think that we'll ever really get a good whack at the truth. Let alone, forty-one.

CHARLES MANSON'S MANIACAL MAYHEM

A unique approach that we took in our aforementioned book *The Beatles, The Bible & Manson* was that in order to lighten the mood in a maniacal menagerie of mass murder we used limericks as a transitional writing motif. Here's a quick clip from the book with a few examples.

As the book title indicates, the music group Manson was most fascinated by was the Beatles. However, the Beach Boys were the group with which Manson was most able to achieve inroads.

This connection begins when, in June of 1968, the Beach Boys' drummer Dennis Wilson picks up the exact same pair of hitchhiking Manson girls for the second time. Feeling like the second consecutive pick-up seems to be more than fate, Dennis brings them back to his Pacific Palisades home.

There once was a Beach Boy named Dennis
Who lived in a beach house in Venice
Surf's Up, California
But Dennis we warn ya
Those hippie chicks can be a menace

In the post-sex conversation banter, Dennis mentions the Beach Boys involvement with Maharishi Mahesh Yogi. Charlie's girls respond by revealing that they too have a guru. Small world, isn't it? Upon meeting, based upon their mutual interest in both sex and music, Dennis and Charlie hit it off and Manson is allowed to move his harem into Dennis' home. Welcome to the summer of '68!

Frivolity immediately ensues, but not for long. By August, this arrangement has cost Dennis $100,000 much of it covering the girls' continual treatment for STD's.

While their practice of mass fornication
Was often a source of elation
Free Love comes with tabs
They found out that crabs
Are more than a kind of crustacean

For any of you who were afraid we would not get through this book without using the word "crustacean" we are glad to have alleviated your fears. For all of you who were hoping we would not get through this book without delving into mass fornication, exult in the fact that we've come through for you. And we're about to come again.

MARILYN CHAMBERS ~ SHE WAS 99 + 44/100 % PURE

Last Halloween we were at our local watering hole, the Cottage Hotel, with our high school buddy Mike McGory, and somebody mentioned the Linda Lovelace piece that was part of an Alice Cooper tribute we had written for the paper the previous Halloween. Just to make sure we're not temporarily losing any readers Googling who these Linda and Alice women are, please allow us to provide the long-story-short for each.

Linda Lovelace was a 1970's porn star most known for her performance in *Deep Throat* (1972). From what we can gather, upon multiple viewings of the film and many personal training sessions, the trick seems to be that it's all about the angle. Alice Cooper was a 1970's rock star who, as you might recall from Chapter 1, is actually a man. Let us clear our throats and move on.

LOVE ON AN ELEVATOR ~ The article we had written for the paper included a story from Alice Cooper's autobiography where, upon performing a concert in Las Vegas in 1973, Alice had received an invitation from Elvis Presley to be his personal guest at his penthouse suite on the top floor of his Vegas hotel. He was assured there would be a private elevator providing transportation from the ground floor to the penthouse suite.

After receiving directions from the hotel desk, Alice proceeded to the location of the private elevator and already waiting there, ready to accompany him to the Elvis suite, was Linda Lovelace. Specific details of the ménage à trois are not included in the book, so we will all have to be left to our collective devices to come up with the succulent specifics on that one. But please keep in mind our previous perspective. It's all about the angle.

The soiree into porn prompted our buddy McGory to suggest that the Marilyn Chambers story might prove to be fruitful fodder for one of our features. We knew there was some kind of connection between Marilyn Chambers and the Ivory Snow detergent box. At the time we were thinking that she appeared on the box as a baby and we planned to look that up when we got home.

The Linda Lovelace/Marilyn Chambers thread led to a collective query amongst us about why, for whatever reason, porn stars used to be able to get famous back in the Golden Age of Porn but nowadays, unless you're able to seduce a President, the names of current adult film actresses don't seem to make it into the mainstream vernacular like they used to be able to do. Turns out there's a reason for that which we'll get to eventually.

IVORY SOAP GIRL ~ So when we get home our research reveals that Marilyn Chambers, (for what it's worth, the #3 female actress on the AVN all-time Top 25 list of female porn stars), was not the baby, she was the mother holding up the baby on the Ivory Snow detergent box. You remember, the one that's 99 + 44/100 percent pure.

It's a very nice picture which is easily accessible on the internet. The advertising goal was to feature an attractively wholesome and loving young mother holding a bright-eyed, adorable baby. Mission accomplished in that regard, and we'll pick up her story from there.

CHANNELING CHAMBERS ~ Marilyn parlayed her modeling success into the respectable beginning of a career in film when she scored a role as Robert Klein's girlfriend in the 1970 film *The Owl and the Pussycat*. Her next movie appearance was in a film called *Together* which was released in 1971. It wasn't nominated for any Academy Awards but it did turn a profit.

Marilyn Chambers' turning point, for better or worse, occurred in 1972 when she responded to a *San Francisco Chronicle* casting call for what was billed as a "major motion picture." Upon responding to the ad she realized it was for a pornographic film called *Behind the Green Door*.

IS THAT CYBIL? ~ Upon realizing what she was about to get herself into, Chambers prepared to leave when the producers, noticing her resemblance to Cybil Shepherd, felt that she was the girl they needed. Subsequently they invited her up to their office, told her the film's plot and considered multiple options to coax her on board.

Marilyn Chambers was highly skeptical about accepting a role in a pornographic film fearing it might ruin her chances of breaking into the mainstream. That being said, she was enticed by the fantasy of the story and decided she would be willing to take a chance of compromising her mainstream goals if she could trade that card for a significant financial cut in the movie deal.

While still an attractive young lady sucked into a shady business, Marilyn Chambers proved early on that she had a good head on her shoulders. Granted this head would be swiveled in multiple directions for multiple purposes but it was a good head nonetheless. She was smart enough to demand a contract that gave her ten percent of the gross receipts for her films.

MEETING MARILYN'S DEMANDS ~ The producers initially balked, but there was a consensus that they needed a lead actress that somehow combined attractively wholesome and provocatively sexy. And they found Chambers' screen tests so adorably arousing that they succumbed and subsequently agreed to fulfill not only her financial demands, but also the requirement that each of her co-stars be tested for STD's.

Right off the bat Chambers displayed a lot of range. *Behind the Green Door* involved lesbian sex, interracial sex, and sex involving a trapeze. How's that for a lot of bridges to cross in one fell swoop? Personally speaking, we've never broken more than two of those taboos in any one given night, but what the hell, we've got time.

Behind the Green Door grossed over $50 million, so with her 10% cut you can do the math regarding Chambers' finances. She made a killing, in a porn film where the movie posters actually billed her as "The All-American Girl Next Door." You gotta love this country. Much of her success was due to perfect timing and it might surprise our readers, but there is a fairly sophisticated film history component attached to this.

GOLDEN AGE OF CHIC ~ The years 1969-1984 are officially referred to as The Golden Age of Porn in film circles and the *New York Times* even coined the phrase "porno chic" to describe the concept. It was the first time that adult films became widely watched by middle America.

In 1973 *The Devil in Miss Jones,* an X-rated film, was actually the seventh highest grossing movie of the year. Mainstream comedians like Johnny Carson and Bob Hope frequently joked about Ivory Snow Girl Marilyn Chambers in their comedy routines.

And how about the Ivory Snow gig in the aftermath of *Behind the Green Door?* When the dots were finally connected on this ironic juxtaposition, Chambers joked, "I bet we sell a lot more soap." While this may have been true, Proctor and Gamble really had no choice but take the politically correct route and come up with a new cover girl for their product.

BASKING IN THE AFTERGLOW ~ So what happened in the aftermath of *Green Door*? Truth be told, not much. Marilyn Chambers spent the rest of the decade trying to cross over into the mainstream film market with limited success. While her goal was certainly a worthy wish, as we all know, if wishes were dollars paupers would be kings. She eventually returned to porn, but by that time the "Golden Era" of the genre was waning, as was her career.

While the adult film world is never going to be seen as the most noble career path, Marilyn Chambers did make it to the top of her field, but we will always choose to remember her most for the 99 + 44/100 percent pure, smiling All-American girl-next-door look from the Ivory Snow box.

BRIGHAM YOUNG'S FAB 55

Mormon evangelist Brigham Young lived part of his young adult life about a mile down the road from us in Mendon, NY. As a matter of fact, his first wife died on September 18, 1832 when he was giving a talk in a barn just around the corner.

The concept of "first wife" takes on a somewhat different perspective within the life of Brigham Young. For the record she was the first of 55 wives. That's a pretty good run by anybody's standards.

In case you're a fan of this type of perversion, we have some fun statistics to share. Brigham Young's most promiscuous year was 1846 when he landed twenty wives. Tim's comment upon seeing this stat, "I can barely keep one woman satisfied, what in the world would I do with twenty!"

HOPES AND FEARS ~ Brigham Young's most promiscuous day was January 28, 1946 when he actually married four women in the same day. And how about the irony of this? Tim's birthday is on January 28th. As Tim's wife, let me go on record with the following statement.

If I were ever able to deliver a birthday present such as Brigham Young's four-wife wedding night, my **greatest hope** would be that he would survive it. And if he did, my **greatest fear** would be, "What the hell do I get him next year?"

CHAPTER 7
DEFTLY DEALING WITH DEATH

HELEN AND HENLEY

This journey will take us to Montreal via Lake Placid, NY. We depart with a somewhat unique connection between these two destinations. Deb's 94-year-old Aunt Helen, who lived in Lake Placid, passed away in 2016. Helen had no relatives in the area except for Deb who was the person who took care of her legal and financial affairs.

Funeral plans were unsettled; at one point some of Deb's family in Virginia were going to come up, but that all fell through and basically, we could just pick a date, drive up, and have the service. So at that point, knowing that we were going to do the 5-hour drive to Lake Placid anyway, and also knowing that Montreal, which we had never been to before, was only two hours away, we got to thinking… let's do Montreal!

So, we googled things to do in Montreal, saw that Don Henley was playing there on September 14th, and picked that date. Yep, the date of Aunt Helen's funeral was determined by the Henley concert. She was always a big Eagles fan, facetiously speaking of course.

ONE FUNNY VISIT ~ One time when we visited Aunt Helen, we had our teenage kids, Skyler and Savanna, with us. We were a little skeptical about how the entire experience would go down because going into any nursing home can be a daunting ordeal, especially for children who may well not have experienced anything like that before.

For a woman in her 90's, Helen was still fairly sharp, but she did have her lapses. However, the silver lining of these lapses was that they were often funnier than hell. Here is a one quick example for you.

HOT TOMATOES ~ On this visit, we all enter her room and find Helen relaxing in her wheelchair in anticipation of our arrival. The first thing Helen does is to share with us her display of tomatoes, which she is proudly showing off on her window sill. The display consists of a fine collection of multiple varieties of tomatoes, and we all share our fascination.

Following that, we roll Helen out into the garden courtyard which features planters that are elevated a few feet above ground level so that wheelchair patients can tend to them. As Tim and the kids are talking to Helen, Deb sees an elderly couple nearby tending their garden. She overhears the wife expressing concern about something and Deb asks if she can help. The wife proceeds to tell us that yesterday there were multiple tomatoes on their vines, but today there are few to be picked.

NCIS EPISODE ~ As our hypothetical crime show "NCIS: Lake Placid" takes over the case, the perp who quickly moves to the top of the suspect list is a white female in her 90's. This may have been the easiest episode ever to solve of "NCIS: Lake Placid." At this point we look at the kids and **we** know, that **they** know, that Helen has picked and pilfered the missing tomatoes. We both give them a look that we hope conveys silence. They pick up on our signals, thus allowing Helen to leave the last crime of her life proudly displayed in the sunshine of her room.

Following Helen's death, we honored her with a very nice service at the Presbyterian Church in Lake Placid. Then we headed to Montreal. If you are an Eagles/Don Henley fan, our following paragraphs here on our dearly departed 94-year-old Aunt Helen might be your favorite ones we've written.

SCREAMING EAGLES ~ During Helen's service, not that we are looking ahead to the Henley concert, but as we reflect back upon the earlier times in Helen's life we realize that "The Heart of the Matter" is that before "The End of the Innocence" changed in a "New York Minute", and "All She Wants to Do is Dance" with "The Boys of Summer", the result was that her "Dirty Laundry" included "Leather and Lace."

But, "I Can't Tell You Why" with "The Long Run" for Helen "Already Gone" with a "Peaceful Easy Feeling", we are not going to "Take it Easy." We are going to check into the "Hotel California", have "One of These Nights", order another "Tequila Sunrise", "Take it to the Limit" and live "Life in the Fast Lane."

FINAL FAREWELL TO A FALLEN FRIEND

Not to be overdramatic about this, but one philosophy that we always try to apply to our lives is to say that the reason God has blessed us with so many wonderful things is that He wants us to take advantage of those blessings and use what we have to bring blessings to others.

We'll lay that out, right here, as the theme of this story. Here we go. On Saturday, July 2, 2017, Tim receives an out-of-the-blue Facebook message from a former student with whom he has not had contact since her graduation in 1994. While it's nice to hear from her, the news isn't good.

She shares that a classmate of hers, and another former student of Tim's, Scott Reese, has stage 4 cancer and is not going to make it through the summer. To compound the problem, Scott and his wife Erin have six kids ranging in age from 2 to 11 years old. She says that one thing she has noticed about us on Facebook is that we seem to have a knack for making special things happen at concerts.

CONCERT REQUEST ~ She doesn't want to seem presumptuous, but if medical arrangements can be worked out, Erin and Scott would like to go see his favorite band, Tom Petty and the Heartbreakers, on their 40th anniversary tour which is coming to town tomorrow night, and she is wondering if we have any connections there to make something special happen.

Well, we really don't, but we've never let that stop us before, so we make it our mission. Upon dialing the phone number for the venue, we immediately encounter our first obstacle. Phone calls only go to voicemail over the weekends and our only option is to leave a message on Facebook and hope someone gets back to us.

So, we compose the most compelling heartfelt version of the story we can and post it. It is hard to be optimistic at this point. After all it is already Saturday afternoon, the concert is the next day, and we can't help but wonder how closely anybody from the venue is going to be monitoring their Facebook page over the weekend. And of course, the follow up question would be … even if somebody does see it, how likely are they to do anything about it?

IN GOD'S HANDS NOW ~ But at this point, a feeling of peaceful resignation sinks in. Even though it doesn't look good, we've done everything we can do. We only had one card we could play in this game and we've played it. So, we go on with our day occasionally checking Facebook. As the day turns into night, hope dwindles for a positive outcome.

After our late workout we decide to check Facebook one last time and lo and behold, we have a message from the venue's head of hospitality. She's embraced our story and they will bless Scott and his wife Erin with VIP treatment.

We are so excited, yet slightly frustrated by the fact that it is too late to share this with anybody, but we go to bed riding a high and looking forward to connecting all the dots in the morning. We are doubly excited because we also have tickets to this sold out concert. So not only have we managed to create a special event for Scott, we are also going to be right there enjoying it with him.

HOLY SCOTT ~ Sunday morning we are up early, establish email contact with Scott, followed by a text message saying, "Hi, Tim & Deb, it's Scott Reese. How have you been? I can't thank you enough for everything you have done for the concert tonight! We are still working on the logistics of everything, but really hope to see you at the show!" Things are coming together.

The next hurdle to climb is that Scott needs to receive medical clearance from his doctors in order to be granted a four-hour hiatus to leave the hospital and attend the concert. Note next how the dominoes begin to fall in this sequence. Hiatus will only be granted if Scott is accompanied by a doctor which the hospital does not have the capacity to provide.

Turns out, Scott's brother Andy is a doctor. Once again, we see God holding His hand over this entire chain of events. As Erin is walking toward the phone to call Andy, the phone rings. It's Andy asking if she needs his help with mowing the lawn today. Erin replies, "I'll swap the lawn favor for another one if you can do it."

She explains the concert situation and Andy is given the option of skipping lawn duty if he is willing to go to the show tonight. That's how life is sometimes; one minute you're planning to pour gas into the lawn mower, and the next minute you're going to see Tom Petty and the Heartbreakers.

ACE IN THE HOLE ~ Making the best of a bad situation, you won't believe the ace Tim seems to have up his sleeve on this one. For a very unique and special reason, Tim thinks he might still have a piece of writing that Scott did in his class 27 years ago. The year was 1990 and for those of you old enough to remember that was about the time when everybody was replacing their vinyl record collections with compact discs.

During that time Rochester's #1 rock radio station had a promotion that aired every afternoon at 4 o'clock called, "The CD Exchange." Listeners were challenged to submit written requests for any specific CD they wanted, one winner was chosen per day, the letter was read on the air, and the CD was awarded. The general task of the writer was to compose something that would stand out because it was funny, or sad, or intriguing for some reason.

So English teacher Tim had an idea. He contacted the radio station and pitched the following proposal to bring his students' writing activities to life. He would give all of his classes the assignment of writing a letter to "The CD Exchange", which would not only count for a writing grade in class, it might perhaps reap real life benefits.

The radio station embraced the mutually symbiotic concept of this annual collaboration between media and education. It was agreed that for one week a year the radio station would feature letters written by Tim's students within the context of their contest.

So as this whole Scott Reese thing is playing out, somewhere deep in the back of Tim's brain, something is telling him that Scott wrote a winning letter which we might still have. We search through his files saved upon retirement, and sure enough, we find a folder of the winning letters for the CD assignment and Scott's winner is there, the original handwritten version dated October 9, 1990.

We are able to bring that letter to the Tom Petty concert and present it to Scott, reminding him of his successful effort back in the glory days of high school. Right now, can anybody cue up Springsteen doing "Glory Days" in the background?

IT'S REALLY HAPPENING ~ Here we leave the letter writing component behind and return to the modern-day storyline. By noon, with Scott's brother on board as the medical support team, things seem to have fallen in place. Keep in mind that this whole process had begun only 24 hours ago. Barring something unforeseen, we are going to be singing Heartbreaker hits with Scott this evening.

Upon departure for the venue, we feel sure we are leaving early enough but our confidence is compromised by a painstakingly slow traffic flow as we approach. That flow is even further impeded when our traffic line grinds to a complete halt to allow the entourage of Tom Petty limousines to skip ahead of us in line. A shallow consolation is that, from our vantage point in the window seat of our shuttle, we are able to name the band members as their limos pass, one-by-one. For the record, no pun intended, in addition to Tom Petty, there were five Heartbreakers.

Upon arrival, and after undergoing the painstaking new security protocol, we head for the VIP tent where we are to meet with head of hospitality. Having been informed that the arrival of the Reese party has been slightly delayed our hostess says, "Come on, let me take you on a walk." This is the walk we described in the first chapter of this book.

We walk back down the hill and return to the VIP tent where we stake out a table for our party to gather at and await the arrival of Scott who is being accompanied by his wife, Erin, and his older brother, doctor Andy. The venue informs us that Scott has arrived, and the staff has initiated the process of transporting him to the VIP tent. We wait for just a few anxious minutes before we see a wheelchair roll through the gates of the tent.

GUEST OF HONOR ~ It's hard to explain the emotions which run through a person in a moment like this. If we had to pick just one word to most accurately describe it, that word would be "paradoxical." Such a twisted combination of exhilarating joy and excruciating agony. Perhaps the most wonderful byproduct of a teaching career is the experience of running into your former students in later years. You just never expect it to be under these circumstances. Therein lies the paradox.

Despite the wheelchair and external ramifications the disease has ravaged upon his body, Tim would have recognized him immediately. The Scott Reese smile has not been compromised by either cancer or chronology and neither has the whit or the humor.

We get to spend about an hour with Scott and his family that evening. Everyone enjoys drinks, dinner and fellowship. After sharing a sneak preview with his wife and brother, Tim presents Scott with the original award-winning letter he had written in Tim's class 27 years earlier. It was a moving experience for everyone involved. Scott leaned over and said to Tim, "I can't thank you enough. You are absolutely the only teacher I ever had that could somehow bring this event together in a day. God bless you."

During dinner our hostess returns to let us know that Scott has the option of watching the entire Tom Petty show on the big screen in the VIP tent, or manning a spot in a special section of the venue. At no surprise to us, given the choice, cancer-stricken Scott chooses to enter the fray and experience the concert with the rest of the fans. As Tom Petty was still proclaiming in one of his anthems, "You Don't **Have** to Live Like a Refugee."

LIFE AND DEATH ~ Some of you may have already been connecting the dots on the timeline of this story. The sad double irony of this saga is that a few months later Scott Reese and Tom Petty would both be dead. As fate would have it, the teaching theme established for the 2017-18 school year at Victor High School where Tim taught was "Teachers Impacting Students' Lives." We were invited to speak about the Scott Reese story and brought Erin along with us. Needless to say, emotions ran high.

We got to visit the Reese household on a few more occasions throughout that summer. The funniest visit of all was when we decided to schedule an interview with all of the kids. We guess that was God's way of having things end on a high note. That would turn out to be the last time we ever saw Scott alive.

We have decided to close out this segment with the following message which Erin posted on Facebook on August 29, 2017.

"At 8:40 pm tonight the most amazing, strong, brave and loving man I will ever know took his last breath in my arms. He fought harder than anyone I know. He is now free from pain and watching over all of us. Scott... I love you with all my heart and always will... Fly high, babe."

CHAPTER 8
HOPING FOR HIGH HOLIDAYS

ALL THE WAY WITH MLK

While giving a shout out to the good doctor for his landmark work with the Civil Rights movement, we are going to honor his memory while sharing with you our two favorite MLK Day stories.

GAYLE KING ~ Our first story comes from *The Late Show with Stephen Colbert* and his guest on this particular show was Oprah Winfrey's best friend and *CBS This Morning* host Gayle King.

Gayle said, "You guys will like this story. There was a time when Martin Luther King Jr. was on the cover of *Time* magazine and, you know, I'm a little kid. I was, like, in fourth grade, and they said something about Martin Luther King and I said, 'Oh, my Uncle Marty!'"

"The teacher said, 'Martin Luther King Jr. is your uncle?' And I said, 'Yes!'"

"So, when my parents came for the parent-teacher conference, my teacher said, 'Oh my god, Mr. King it's an honor to meet you. The work your brother is doing . . . 'And my father says, 'Beauregard and Jerome?'"

"My teacher then said, 'No, Martin Luther King Jr.'"

"My parents just sat there in stunned silence. Of course, I got in trouble. That was my first introduction to the concept that it's not good to tell a lie!"

CHRIS ROCK ~ Next, we'll maintain the Late Night theme and channel surf over to *Late Night with David Letterman*. One night his guest was Chris Rock and the topics of Martin Luther King Jr. and Oprah Winfrey were prominent in Rock's comedy banter.

We are going to go directly to the transcript for this part.

> **Dave**: You and Oprah are friends; I know you've traveled with Oprah as a matter of fact.
>
> **Chris**: I went to the opening of her school.
>
> **Dave**: In South Africa?

Chris: Yes, yes. (pauses, then sarcastically) I noticed you weren't there Dave.

Dave: No. But I'll tell you something. I love Oprah and I'd like to weasel my way in and get closer to her.

Chris: Oprah is an amazing person. She's close to being a superhero. Almost, you know what I mean? Cause she can get away with things that a normal human being could never get away with. Like Oprah's got her own magazine, called *Oprah* magazine and she's on the cover every month.

Dave: Every month.

Chris: I couldn't get away with such an act. If I had a *Chris Rock* magazine and I was on the cover every month people would be going, "Who the hell does he think he is?" And I love it, I look forward to it. I love the magazine. I read it every month and I look forward to the picture because she always has a different pose. It's like Oprah playin' football (does Heisman Trophy pose), Oprah ridin' a horse (makes galloping pose), Oprah poppin' a wheelie (grabs pretend handlebars). You know I love it so much that if somebody else is on the cover I get mad. Like even if Martin Luther King Jr. was on the cover, I'd go, "What the hell has he done to be on the cover of *Oprah* magazine?" That Dream was a long time ago, Dave, right?" That's what I'd say.

Dave: You're pretty sure people have your email address, right?

SALACIOUSLY CELEBRATING ST. PATRICK'S DAY

The list of four geographic locations where St. Patrick's Day is an official holiday is a bit quirky. You have the two fairly obvious entries, the countries of Ireland and Northern Ireland, and the list is completed by the Canadian province of Newfoundland and the Caribbean island of Montserrat (More on these last two later – both good stories). All the rest of us are celebrating unofficially. But that doesn't mean we can't have fun.

On a worldwide basis St. Patrick's Day has become a general celebration of Irish heritage which has come to encompass many folks who have no Irish heritage whatsoever. Countries which rank high on the list of celebrating the day include the U.S., Canada, Great Britain, Australia, New Zealand and Argentina, which perhaps surprisingly, other than Ireland, has the 5th largest Irish population in the world.

NEWFOUNDLAND ~ This Canadian province, officially titled "Newfoundland and Labrador", boasts the provincial motto of "The Most Irish Place in the World Outside of Ireland." And they take their St. Patrick's Day event very seriously, so seriously in fact that it lasts five days.

It also comes with a double bonus. The festivities begin on the last Monday before March 17th and run for five days. So depending on the calendar, in some years the original 5-day event could end **before** St. Patrick's Day, in which case you get a bonus day because the most Irish place in the world is going to celebrate on March 17th even if the original 5-day event is over.

George Street, the main drag in Newfoundland's capital of St. John's, has the most bars and pubs per square foot of any place in North America. As their website brags, when you are partying in St. John's, "You are not bar hopping so much as stumbling another 10 feet."

MONTSERRAT ~ Talk about an island with a story to tell, they don't get much more bizarre than what has happened to this British territory in the Caribbean. Hitting first upon the reason why Montserrat is the southernmost place in the world to observe St. Patrick's Day as an official holiday, the island was originally settled by Irish refugees and is nicknamed the "Emerald Island of the Caribbean." It's a beautiful nickname which describes, or used to describe, the beauty of the island.

On a more recent note, Montserrat has also been nicknamed the "Modern Day Pompeii." On July 18, 1995 a volcano erupted leaving two-thirds of the island as an uninhabitable "exclusion zone." There are kitchen tables still set exactly the way they were that morning in 1995 when the inhabitants had to spontaneously flee their homes with no warning whatsoever. So our stance on the situation is that if anybody needs to drink, it's these poor folks … if they want every day be St. Patrick's Day then we say let them go for it.

FINAL FUN FACT ~ St. Patrick … Neither Irish nor named Patrick … He was born in England and before sainthood went by the name Maewyn Succat.

DETERMINING THE DATE OF EASTER

Welcome to the shortest segment of our book. We saw a poll that said the number of people who knew, off the top of their heads, the formula for determining the date of Easter was only 15%. That led us to the decision that a worthwhile Easter chapter could be just to inform folks of the formula to figure out when the holiday falls.

For the record, the earliest Easter could be is March 22 and on the other end of the spectrum it can be as late as April 25. What is the formula that results in such a wide range of possibilities? Easter falls on the first Sunday, after the first full moon, after the first day of spring. If you miss church next year don't blame it on us.

DOUBLING DOWN ON DYNGUS DAY

ANDERSON COOPER ~ If you happen to be at your computer right now, before you even start this component we urge you to do the following. Go to YouTube, and type in "Anderson Cooper Dyngus Day." You'll see the words "giggle fit" automatically added to the line. Cue it up because it is absolutely hilarious and once you see this video our prediction is that you'll pick this book back up even more quickly than you put it down.

Cooper is doing a spot on Dyngus Day within the "Ridiculist" segment of his show and when he gets to the part where he is describing the girls hitting the boys with their wet pussy willows, he absolutely loses it. It takes a full one minute and twelve seconds for him to get through his giggle fit and regain his composure.

The aforementioned segment before and after the giggles also provides a nice little nutshell background to Dyngus Day, the early origins of which can be traced back to 966 A.D. when Poland's first king Mieszko was baptized into Christianity thus bringing Catholicism to that country. If you can't go to the video right now, please allow us to provide you with our best one-sentence summary. Falling on the Monday after Easter, Dyngus Day is to Poland what St. Patrick's Day is to Ireland; just like everybody's Irish on St. Patrick's Day, everybody's Polish on Dyngus Day.

IT'S BETTER IN BUFFALO ~ By happenstance, we ironically and fortunately find ourselves in prime position to provide precise firsthand coverage of the largest Dyngus Day celebration in the world. While the Polish-American holiday of Dyngus Day is celebrated to various degrees in multiple countries around the world, for some quirky, fateful reasons the largest annual Dyngus Day debauchery on the globe occurs near us in Buffalo, NY. We went last year. We lived it, we loved it, and here's our report.

To use an analogy which appropriately takes advantage of the food for which the city is most known, Buffalo has taken Dyngus Day under its wings. While strolling the streets amongst the 100,000 people who attend annually, we observe the romantic Dyngus Day foreplay consisting of girls whipping boys with wet pussy willows amidst the simultaneous exchange of ejaculated Easter water from squirt bottles and guns. We could draw you a road map of the sexual euphemisms conveyed by this imagery, but we're thinking conclusions could come on your own.

And then there's the parade, which is like no other. Fueled by Polish pride and perhaps a little vodka, there's an almost-anything-goes atmosphere as the floats wend their way through the parade route. The destination is the Pussy Willow Park Party Tent where drinks are a-flowin' on while dancing is a-goin' on.

The fact that Buffalonians have managed to establish the greatest Dyngus Day tradition in the world has become a concept that feeds upon itself. The pride it instills fosters the participation of even more people which in turn intensifies the tradition. It's a cycle that continues to trend upward. Buffalonians have embraced this day as their own and the holiday has embraced the city in return.

HOLIDAY COMPARISONS ~ In drawing holiday analogies we previously used the formula of St. Patrick's Day → Ireland = Dyngus Day → Poland. However, another worthy comparison for Dyngus Day would be Mardi Gras' Fat Tuesday and from a calendar perspective the analogy is obvious.

Fat Tuesday is the day before Lent begins (Ash Wednesday) and Dyngus Day is the day after Lent ends (Easter Sunday). So each of those holidays serves the purpose of allowing the participants to blow off steam just before and just after a period of sacrifice.

IN SUMMARY ~ The springtime concept of starting over is something that humans celebrate regardless of cultural background. The wonder of watching nature come back to life after months of dormancy is something that never tires, regardless of one's age or experience. The satisfaction that comes with the warmth associated with longer days and shorter nights causes quirky celebrations all across the globe.

As we said, these days everybody's Polish on Dyngus Day. And although this peculiar party is spreading throughout the nation, there's no other place in the world to more ceremoniously celebrate the end of Lent than the "Dyngus Day Capital of the World," Buffalo, New York.

As the only place that could cause Anderson Cooper to laugh his ass off beyond anything in comparison within his well-respected broadcast career, Buffalo be blessed. It's where Dyngus Day is not just a day, it's a state of mind.

A HAUNTING HALLOWEEN

THE JOKE'S ON US ~ Our Halloween present for you this year is going to be a joke. Here we go … Cory Dupree, a tourist in Vienna, is going past Vienna's Zentralfriedhof Graveyard on October 31st. All of a sudden, he hears some music. No one is around, so he starts searching for the source. Cory finally locates the origin and finds it is coming from a grave with a headstone that reads: Ludwig van Beethoven, 1770-1827. Then he realizes that the music is Beethoven's Ninth Symphony and it is being played backward! Puzzled, he leaves the graveyard and persuades Sarah Barker, a friend, to return with him.

By the time they arrive back at the grave, the music has changed. This time it is the Seventh Symphony, but like the previous piece, it is being played backward. Curious, Cory and Sarah agree to consult a music scholar. When they return with the expert, the Fifth Symphony is playing, again backward. The expert notices that the symphonies are being played in the reverse order in which they were composed, the 9th, then the 7th, then the 5th.

As word of the Halloween phenomena spreads and evening approaches, a throng has gathered around the grave and now they are all listening to the Third Symphony, being played backward. Just then the graveyard's caretaker ambles up to the group. Someone in the crowd asks him if he has an explanation for the music playing at Beethoven's grave.

"Oh, it's nothing to worry about," says the caretaker. "Oddly, he's just decomposing!"

THANKSGIVING TRUTHS

Few holidays in the calendar year are more steeped in tradition than Thanksgiving. For what it's worth however, the historical accuracy behind many of these traditional stories ranges from loose to nonexistent. For example…

TOPIC #1 ~ THE FIRST THANKSGIVING ~ The go-to story that we all pretty much grew up with was set in Plymouth, Massachusetts in 1621 and starred the Pilgrims and the Indians sharing a meal. Well, truth be told, the whole gig originally went down two years before in Virginia with the alteration that the invites to the Indians apparently got lost in the mail. This was an all-white gala with 38 attendees which occurred on December 4, 1619 in the newly established British colony of Berkeley on the James River.

The colonists' ship had landed that day and the event was more about prayers than potatoes, but there is a surviving document stipulating that the day of their arrival "shall be yearly and perpetually kept holy as a day of Thanksgiving to Almighty God." Now they probably did not submit the paperwork to copyright the term Thanksgiving, but there it is, complete with a capital "T" indicating its usage as a proper noun. And while there are no surviving menus from the dinner it probably would have consisted of seafood and ham (wild boar).

Certainly, a contributing factor to this acknowledgement of Thanksgiving not being the one that became most recognized was apparently the Indians had a different vision for what was meant by "perpetually" than the colonists had. In March of 1622, perhaps as part of a St. Patrick's Day celebration gone terribly awry, the Indians attacked Berkeley and killed most of the colonists, thus America's first Thanksgiving was virtually lost to history.

TOPIC #2 ~ THE MENU ~ Let's return to Plymouth, Massachusetts and take a look at the traditional perception of what went down at that first New England version of Thanksgiving. Here is a list of traditional holiday food staples totally missing from the menu at Thanksgiving #1. There was no turkey, stuffing, potatoes, or cranberries. The Indians provided the Pilgrims with five deer and the meal was completed with shellfish, berries, and boiled pumpkin. Please pass the whipped cream.

FUN FACT AND A JOKE ~ In 1953, Swanson overestimated the number of frozen turkeys that it would sell on Thanksgiving by 26 tons. The company decided to slice up the extra meat and repackage it – creating the first-ever TV dinners.

Here's a quick joke that you can tell at your Thanksgiving dinner this year: A lady was looking through the frozen turkeys at the grocery store, but couldn't find one big enough for her family. She asked the stock boy, "Do these turkeys get any bigger?" The stock boy answered, "No ma'am, they're dead."

CHRISTMAS ISLAND IS THE REAL DEAL

For the Christmas segment of our holiday chapter we're going to take you on a trip to Christmas Island and do some fact checking on the lyrics of the classic song. By the end of this you're going to be able to make an informed decision as to whether you really would like to spend Christmas there, or not. We love the story of this island.

Christmas Island is an Australian territory located in the Indian Ocean about halfway between India and Australia. A full 63% of the 52-square-mile island is dedicated to a national park and the diverse topography features everything from a rain forest to wetlands to waterfalls. A unique array of flora and fauna populate the island along with about 1,600 people. The island is ringed with snorkeling and diving reefs.

LAST INHABITED PLACE ON EARTH - One significant contributing factor as to why Christmas Island turned out to be such a beautiful and unique place is that it was literally the last habitable island in the world to become inhabited. When Britain claimed the island in 1887, there was not a soul on it. In 1897 they began to plot a strategy for the development of the island. Step one in this process was that an expedition, led by Charles Andrews, spent ten months on the island from mid-1897 to mid-1898.

The bottom line was that they thought things through before settling and developing the island and took the time to do it right. The expedition produced a 359-page volume documenting the island's flora, fauna, and geographical features.

In his introduction, Andrews stated his mission as follows: "It seemed highly desirable that this interesting island should be carefully examined and described by a competent naturalist and geologist before being opened up by Europeans for agricultural and commercial purposes in that it is the only existing island never inhabited by man, savage or civilized."

Another way of restating Andrews' summary would be to say that of any piece of land on the planet where people actually live today, Christmas Island was the last place to become inhabited. So on the whole, Christmas Island is blessed with a nice combination of natural beauty and personal planning.

THE SONG CHRISTMAS ISLAND ~ Next let's apply the theorem of the plausible impossible to fact check some of the lyrics of the "Christmas Island" song. Most of the lyrics are fairly generic and don't lend themselves to the concept of fact checking, but here are the ones that do.

"Let's get away from sleigh bells, let's get away from snow."
There's no law against sleigh bells, so some troublemaker could conceivably smuggle some of those in, but the escape from snow is a sure thing. The temperature never drops below 60° on Christmas Island.

"How'd ya like to hang your stocking on a great big coconut tree?"
This would be easy; those trees are all over the damn place.

"How'd ya like to stay up late, like the islanders do?"
Well, you may be staying up by yourself. The island is not known for late night partying.

"Wait for Santa to sail in with your presents in a canoe."
Even if you are a true believer, this one's probably not gonna happen. In all likelihood Santa will be taking the sleigh on this run due to logistical circumstances. The closest possible location from which Santa could launch his canoe would be 310 miles away at the southwestern tip of Indonesia. In order for this to actually happen Santa would probably have to start paddling shortly after Thanksgiving, clearly shirking his many pre-holiday obligations.

"For every day your Christmas dreams come true."
Our take on this would be that if you could snap your fingers and be there it sounds like a tropical paradise with a tantalizing appeal. But the logistics certainly present a challenge; the only flights in emanate from Australia. So for most of us we may just have to rely on the magic of Christmas and see if we can hitch a ride in on Santa's sleigh.

CHAPTER 9
TITILLATING TRAVEL TALES

JUSTIFYING THE JIM THORPE THEFT

WHAT'S IN A NAME? ~ Of all the locations we have ever visited, here is our very best story regarding the naming of a place. Please join us in a somewhat creepy convoy to the Keystone State. Located deep in the heart of Pennsylvania is the picturesque town of Jim Thorpe. As one might suspect the town is named after the famous athlete, but the circumstances of how the town came to bear Jim Thorpe's name bizarrely border on the morbidly macabre.

Prior to Thorpe's death in 1953, the town was called Mauch Chunk. We kid you not. We challenge you to come up with two words and ten letters with a less appealing sound. The beauty and curse of that name is how it manages to get so ugly so quick. For example, if you wave the limit on letters you could come up with a two-word alternative name that might seem to mean about the same thing. How about "Projectile Vomiting," PA? Is there any way we could have a name that was **less** marketable?

So, any way you want to cut the Mauch Chunk cheese, this town is cursed with one of the ugliest sounding names ever. So, what do the Mauch Chunkians do with their pukey Pennsylvania persona? Obviously, it was going to take some initiative and ingenuity to dig out of that valley. They already have a truly picturesque town nestled amidst the peaks of the Pocono Mountains, and they come to the conclusion that their trending tourist trade could be terrifically touted if the town's name could be changed to have the travel brochures **not** sound like potential visitors need to bring their own vomit bags.

TIME FOR A CHANGE ~ So, in order to set itself apart from the many other sleepy villages that dot the Poconos, Mauch Chunk feels it needs a name-changing/game-changing gimmick. What follows is a unique example of how quirkily the universe sometimes aligns. We're halfway through the 20th century, the country is getting back on track after World War II, Mauch Chunk is looking for a new name, and legendary athlete Jim Thorpe dies.

How in the world do these dots connect? Well, the details of the negotiations are a bit murky but the long-story-short of it is that Jim Thorpe's widow, who was **not** the mother of any of his 8 children, agrees to sell her husband's corpse to Mauch Chunk for an undisclosed amount of money. The idea is that the town would entomb the body, erect the ultimate shrine for the sports legend, and rename the town "Jim Thorpe"; all of this despite the fact that Thorpe had never even personally been there.

Overlooking the objection of everyone else in Thorpe's family, as well as the obvious moral and ethical issues, Thorpe's wife did have the legal right to conduct this transaction. Thorpe's family has tried unsuccessfully from 1953 to this very day to have his remains returned to his native Oklahoma where they could be more appropriately buried. But the residents of the old Mauch Chunk obviously felt that the one-time expense of everybody having to ante up and buy new address labels was well worth it. They are keeping the body and keeping the name.

GREATEST OF ALL TIME ~ Jim Thorpe is considered by some to be the greatest athlete of all time. He played Major League Baseball and was also an early star in the NFL. Track and field may have been his best sport but he was great at everything from ballroom dancing to riding horses.

The opinion of who is the greatest athlete ever could be debated indefinitely with valid cases to be made for multiple candidates. But we are going to go out on a limb and, greatest athlete debate notwithstanding, we are going to say that without a doubt the greatest single year ever experienced by an all-around athlete was what Jim Thorpe accomplished in 1912.

In the spring of that year he won the college ballroom dancing championship (who would have thought that they even had such a thing at that time?). In the summer he sailed to Stockholm and won the Olympic gold medals in both the pentathlon and decathlon. He then returned home in the fall to lead his team to the national collegiate football championship. How's that for having a good year?!

Of course, the real glory was still awaiting him when 50 years later a small town in Pennsylvania would come to bear his name.

THE PERPETUATION OF
PERVASIVE PARTYING IN PEEKSKILL

POPPING IN TO PEEKSKILL ~ Sometimes our adventures start out modestly and just snowball into craziness. Case in point ... we had this notion that we wanted to go see the first band we ever saw together back in high school. The fruition of that notion ends up culminating in a two-day trip to Peekskill, NY, a surprise tour of West Point, the warmest February day in the history of New York State and a late-night celebration of Olympic hockey gold with a convention of wild U.S. Army recruiters. And all that was just the first day!

The very first concert we ever saw was the group Three Dog Night and as we check their 2018 tour schedule the closest we see them coming to us is a performance in Peekskill which is on the other side of the state from us, a 5-hour drive away. While we're talking geography, we'll throw in the fact West Point is only 13 miles from Peekskill which will help connect the dots in our previous paragraph.

As we contemplate this concert, the next day we notice our favorite 1990's group, the Gin Blossoms have been booked to play the previous night at the same venue. At this point "Hey Jealousy" it's a five-hour drive but "Joy to the World" let's go for it. In that order.

Having bravely booked this binge many months ago, the danger of winter weather had lurked in the back of our minds but this two-day February foray launches with the mildest weather forecast we could hope for. We arrive in Peekskill, check in, and head to the hotel lobby to set up shop and write because you never know what you might stumble upon, or perhaps what might stumble upon you.

As the afternoon progresses, we notice a Peekskill pattern establish itself amongst the people checking in. There is a preponderance of large muscular men, most adorned with tattoos, and all sporting military haircuts. We realize there has to be a connection in place here, and as some of the men begin to return to the lobby and congregate, we approach one group and ask what they're here for.

Turns out we are sharing quarters with the semiannual convention of the Albany Area Army Recruitment Officers. We tell them that we write for our local paper, we're always looking for a story, and we'd like to hear theirs. It actually turns out to be a pretty good one; not quite as good as the stories we would be hearing from them later at one o'clock in the morning, but good nonetheless.

Here's the purpose of this convention. These guys are from a four-state area which includes eastern New York, western Massachusetts, Connecticut, and Vermont, and they get together twice a year to share recruiting strategies.

RUNNING JOKE ~ As we circulate through the lobby for the next couple hours, we are clearly taken under their Army wings. Next, we'll share the storyline that becomes the running joke which characterizes our time with these guys throughout this afternoon. The Army's team-building agenda for the recruiters this night includes a women's basketball game at West Point between Army and Colgate.

As the afternoon progresses, the Army recruiters approach us with escalating offers of enticements to trade our Gin Blossoms tickets for their tickets to the Army/Colgate girls' hoops game. Of course it is all in jest, but when we hear the offer come up for lifetime tickets to the Army/Navy football game it does temporarily give us cause to pause.

FIELD TRIP TO WEST POINT ~ As we manage to successfully hang on to our concert tickets, word comes down that since the weather is so freakishly warm, some of the troops decide that a mission to West Point is in order. As the recruiters' new best friends, and perhaps not coincidentally the only people in the house with tickets to the Gin Blossoms, we are offered the opportunity to sign on for the field trip to West Point. Having never been to West Point, getting a firsthand tour with a team of experts, was obviously quite an experience. The campus and the buildings there are historically beautiful. With the balmy February temperatures hitting a record-breaking 70°, we couldn't have hoped for anything more.

LATER THAT NIGHT ~ So after returning to the hotel, our two parties divert paths. While the Army attendees soldier forth to the Colgate game, the Smiths grab their concert gear and head for the Gin Blossoms. After a great show we walk unassumingly back into our hotel around 10:45 to grab one last nightcap at the bar. Upon entry, we hear our names ringing out from the Army recruiters who we had met earlier in the day. We feel like Norm walking into the bar at Cheers. History never repeats itself ... but it often rhymes.

The Army women's basketball game against Colgate, which the recruiters basically had to attend, obviously ended a while before our concert because they have clearly been here for some time. Better yet, or perhaps worse yet, at this point they are only priming their pumps for the U.S. Olympic women's hockey team gold medal game against Canada which is scheduled to start at 11:10 pm on February 21, 2018. The phrase "Let the games begin" never had a better double meaning.

At this point Deb turns to Tim and says, "Thank God we're not teaching anymore. This night might turn out to be a long one." For any of our readers who were truly hanging on the thread of the Army/Colgate women's basketball game, we are informed that the final score was 69-49, Black Knights over Red Raiders.

DAYTON & EATON ~ Our informant happens to be wearing a Dayton Flyers t-shirt which prompts us to ask if he went to college at Dayton and lead to one of the more memorable lines of the night. The guy tells us yes, and shares that he grew up in the town of New Lebanon, Ohio which is halfway between Dayton and Eaton. At this point we have set the guy up for a joke he has clearly told before.

He goes on to tell us that it was tough as a kid growing up in New Lebanon. We do our part and ask him why. He says, "Here's the reason it's tough to grow up in a small town halfway between Dayton and Eaton. Whenever I went out with a girl I could never remember if I was datin' a girl from Eaton, or eatin' a girl from Dayton." Meanwhile, back to the hockey game.

PERIOD 1 ~ As the first puck is dropped, a somewhat surrealistic sense of celebration sweeps through us. Here we are on the warmest February day ever in New York State, surrounded by dozens of Army officers, about to watch the U.S. women try to win their first gold medal in two decades. The scenario certainly reflects the convergence of some unique factors. Suffice it to say it was an exuberantly effusive endeavor and if you could get your hands on the security footage, we guarantee it would go viral on YouTube.

The first period ends on an encouraging note; the U.S. has tallied the first goal and heads to the locker room with a 1-0 lead. Somebody proposes the concept that every time a U.S. shot goes in, we match it with a shot of our own. The crowd capitulates to the concept, all knowing of course this treatise has the potential to go terribly, terribly astray.

But the only person taking notes at this point is Deb and there's a strong feeling that anything she's composing this night will never hold up in court anyway. Perhaps the saddest aspect of this whole situation is that Deb has now assumed the unofficial position of 5-star den mother. Doesn't pay a lot, but you gotta love the company. The second period is a sobering affair; Canada scores two goals to take a 2-1 lead into the locker room.

We become a tight knit group rallying around the flag in the hotel bar that Wednesday night; it is pretty much just the bartenders, the Smiths, and the GI Joes. There are a couple of the Army leaders subtly trying to keep a bit of a lid on things, but when concerns are raised that the crowd may be getting too boisterous, one officer accurately puts things in perspective. He says, "The bartender just told me that they've already broken their sales record for a weekday night, so there's no way the hotel is going to shut down this festival!"

With our crowd energized and optimistically anticipating a U.S. comeback for Olympic gold, the puck is dropped to begin period three. But the optimism is admittedly starting to wane when the clock ticks below the seven-minute mark with the Canadians still clinging to their 2-1 lead.

And then it happens, the U.S. ties the game and the place goes blissfully berserk. Fortunately for the hotel, and we suppose our group of cohorts as well, the bar is located at one end of the hotel and there is a large lobby area in between us and the nearest hotel patrons. And there is a final crescendo of cheers when the U.S. ultimately goes on to win the game in a shoot-out, and take home the gold.

At that point, all the hard cores who stayed up for the whole game begin moseying back to their rooms and the next morning there are some tired looking GI Joe's bellying up to the waffle bar at the breakfast buffet.

HONEYMOON HISTRIONICS

We went to Disney World on our honeymoon and wrote a six-week series for the paper about our tour of the World Showcase in Epcot. We wrote a component on all 11 nations represented in the showcase and we're going to pick our two favorite segments to share with you here. Only the best for our faithful readers.

NORWEGIAN CRUISE ~ Let's go to Norway first. We visit the Norway pavilion on consecutive days which proves fortuitous because this story would not have come together had we not returned the following day. Upon entering Norway on day #1, we patronize the cold water bottle kiosk by the pavilion entrance which is being operated by a kid in a Norway soccer jersey.

As fate would have it, this day would be a date that would live in infamy in the history of Norway soccer and the kid we speak to is clearly a soccer fan. When he notices Tim is wearing a U.S. World Cup jersey, they immediately connect. On that day Norway had lost a World Cup qualifying match to Liechtenstein and the Norway kid is beside himself.

"Liechtenstein," he laments, "who knew they even had a freakin' team?" So the boys bond over a little soccer talk with Tim consoling the kid and assuring him there would be better days. "Look at the bright side," Tim teases upon our departure, "maybe you guys could book a match with the Vatican City or Monaco."

That could have been the end of the story, but no no, never in Norway. When we lap the World Showcase the next night, the cold water kid is again stationed at the Norway entrance. And he is waiting for us in a calculated demeanor of deprecation.

Lamenting the lowly Liechtenstein loss, the kid is clearly down on his team. He rattles off half a dozen one-liners and we'll share our favorite three with you right here.

Q: What is the difference between a dead dog in the road and a dead Norway soccer player?
A: Skid marks in front of the dog.

Q: What do you call a Norwegian in the World Cup Final?
A: A referee.

Q: What does Cinderella and the Norwegian soccer team have in common?
A: They both keep running away from the ball.

At least if you're going to lose a bad one, best to be able to accept the loss with an element of humor.

MARRAKESH EXPRESS ~ Next, we're going to "Play it Again, Sam" and visit Morocco for the final component of our honeymoon piece. We just thought that this story deliriously demonstrated Darwin's survival theory as applied to plants. Our visit to Morocco happens to coincide with the daily guided tour of the gardens and, holy shit, do we luck out! Read on for that x-rated expression to totally christen the crapper.

The vegetation is lush and beautiful in Morocco and our tour blesses us with one fun fact we feel completely compelled to share. Turns out growing bananas is a mainstay of Moroccan agriculture. And those banana trees are a lot smarter than you think. Check this out.

Banana trees have a unique strategy to assure propagation. They just don't leave their seeds scattered around on the ground. Why? Because some animal might come by and eat the seeds, or later step on the young sprouts. So the genetic survival plan of the banana tree is to strategically implant its seeds within the bananas themselves.

Upon first thought that might seem like a flawed plan. The obvious question would be, "How does the entire banana get itself into the ground?" And the answer would be that it doesn't. What happens is that a monkey or some other animal eats the banana, the fruit is digested by the animal, the seeds sprout inside the animal's body, and subsequently hit the forest floor with an organic splat.

Wow! There's your baby banana tree, right in its own pile of fertilizer. Nobody is going to step on it and even a warthog knows better than to eat something growing out of a pile of monkey dung. It's a brilliant strategy for survival and propagation. But next time you have a banana don't spend too much time worrying about where the seeds have been.

CHAPTER 10
MAKING MUSICAL MEMORIES

SURF'S UP WITH THE BEACH BOYS

Since high school we have always been bona fide Beach Boys fans. Collectively we've seen them well over 100 times and know the band members, some better than others. Subsequently, we felt we would be remiss if we didn't share our most rad story about achieving cred with the actual boys in "America's Band."

Tim's initial connection with the Beach Boys was established in the early 1980's when, in his capacity of being our town's recreation director, he submitted a photo to the band which they decided to use on the inside cover of their 1985 self-titled album *The Beach Boys*. The picture featured 45 kids from our town's summer recreation program laying out on beach towels spelling out the band's iconic logo.

SUMMER OF 2015 - Things gradually expanded from there and we'll fast forward three decades to our most bodacious Beach Boys binge. During the summer of 2015 as concert dates were gradually announced, a summer tour came together where we, along with our friends Andrew and Karen, were going to be seeing the band perform on four days, in four different states. The fours are wild.

Now the states were all in New England, so once we got there the daily travel was not as significant as you might have suspected. The actual state order was Connecticut, New Hampshire, Rhode Island, Massachusetts.

We have been backstage often enough that even the senior leaders of the band, Mike Love and Bruce Johnston, recognize us. It's not like they would know our names if you asked them, but when we manage to get invited backstage during the afternoon of the third day of our sojourn, Mike and Bruce look at us, know they have seen us before, and Bruce jokingly comments, "Hey Guys, great to see you again. Do you remember us?"

Of course, the irony of the joke is that line should go the other way around.

This afternoon turns out to be one of the most memorable of our lives. Here we are sitting on the ocean, at the Newport Beach Yacht Club on a hot summer day, sipping coconut vodka with the Beach Boys.

When they hear the details of our four-day, four-state travelogue they thank us for our dedication and support, and tell us that since we have made the effort to go four-for-four they want to make it five-for-five and they bless us with front center tickets for what will make it our fifth concert in five days. Surf's Up!!!

PARTYING WITH THE PARROTHEADS

On our honeymoon we flew to Disney World for three days before renting a car and driving to West Palm Beach to see Jimmy Buffett. After gallivanting with Goofy, it was definitely time for a Cheeseburger in Paradise. We arrived early because as you may know, in one of the greatest leaps of life since the amphibians hit the beach in the Paleozoic Era, the parking lot at a Jimmy Buffett concert, in and of itself, is almost as sensational as the show.

Of course, the Dead Heads were around first, but the Parrotheads have probably taken the concept of tailgating to a more sophisticated level. One factor behind this is that Parrotheads generally tend to be more professional, and have more resources available to them. This can be a little scary because you know that some of the people you see going crazy in the parking lot on Saturday night may well be handling your health or finances on Monday morning.

In honor of the event we wrote the following poem which was actually the very first poem we had published. Once you get started with that poetry writing, it can become hard to stop as evidenced by this book. But here's our debut; the one where we lost our poetic virginity so to speak.

It's Jimmy Buffett Day in town
He comes here once a year
The Parrotheads will soon abound
As will the kegs of beer

For antics in the parking lot
You've got the Grateful Dead
But if you want to be the best
Become a Parrothead

Don your grass skirts, don your fins
And fire up the blender
Add the booze and add the fruit
And see what it will render

Ditch the business suits today
And grab your pirate hat
Get cobwebs off your coconut bra
You'll have some fun in that

Decorate your van or car
Party till you get your fill
Join the fun because you are
In Margaritaville

So now that the tailgating is done, it is time for the show. Everyone order a "Boat Drink," grab a "Cheeseburger in Paradise," and prepare to have the "Son of a Son of a Sailor" take you away to an evening in "Margaritaville." Final thought, while departing, hope that, "Come Monday," the doctors and lawyers you step over on the way out are not the ones showing up to perform surgery on you, or represent you in court.

DARK SIDE OF THE RAINBOW

FLOYD MEETS OZ ~ One of the more unique rock 'n roll legends in circulation is the connection between Pink Floyd's *Dark Side of the Moon* album and the classic 1939 film *The Wizard of Oz*. We're sure a portion of our readers might be familiar with this storyline, but if you're not, here's the scoop.

If you correctly cue up the beginning of the movie with the beginning of the album there is a truly amazing array of connections between the lyrics of the album and the action in the movie. Pivotal scenes eerily appear to coincide with the end of one track and the beginning of the next.

Alternate titles have been applied to the analysis of this phenomenon such as *The Dark Side of Oz* and *Dorothy Meets the Dark Side* but we're going to use *Dark Side of the Rainbow*. It's actually not that we necessarily like this one best, but when we send you to the internet to conduct this experiment on your own, the title of the video you will need to locate is *Popular Videos - Dark Side of the Rainbow,* so that's what we're going with.

So, did Pink Floyd intentionally sync their *Dark Side of the Moon* album to *The Wizard of Oz* movie or was it all just one crazy coincidence? It's a great topic to explore because there is not an ironclad yes or no answer to the question, and if you follow the directions, we will provide you in this piece, you'll enjoy an experience that is truly mind-blowing at points, no matter what decision you may settle on.

The first documented reference to this *Dark Side of the Rainbow* phenomenon was on a Pink Floyd online forum in 1995 and the whole sensation didn't attract nationwide attention until 1997 when a Boston DJ brought it to the attention of a larger audience. At that point the whole thing went viral, even reaching the level where Turner Movie Classics aired *The Wizard of Oz* in 2000 with *Dark Side of the Moon* as an alternate audio option.

PLANNED OR COINCIDENCE? ~ So, to use a trendy modern-day word, allow us to pose the question, "Was there collusion in the creation of *Dark Side of the Moon*?" It is our goal to share with you all the pertinent facts and allow you to come to your own collusion conclusion. An aspect of this debate that adds to the appeal is that excellent arguments can be made for both opinions and it makes for a damn fine piece of entertainment, coincidence or not.

Okay fans, coming up will be your step-by-step directions to experience this phenomenon and decide if it was a magnificent master plan or a complete coincidence.

In order to achieve the utmost synchronicity, the album should be cued up to start when the MGM lion **finishes** his third roar during the opening sequence. You have to be sure to sync this perfectly or it won't "work."

If you're like us, this was the kind of film that you watched religiously once a year as a kid, but you may not have cued it up recently. When we were kids, and there were only three networks, *The Wizard of Oz* aired once annually, usually around Halloween. Nowadays, with a million cable channels and DVD availability, you can watch the *Wizard* whenever you want.

If our introduction has enticed you into experiencing this entertainment extravaganza on your own, please allow us to continue upon our never-ending mission to inform as well as entertain. There is actually a video available on YouTube that does all the heavy lifting for you. So why not cue it up and have some fun? Play-by-play directions now follow.

YOUR DIRECTIONS ~ Here are your Tim & Deb directions which will enable you to enjoy this unique experience. Enter "Dark Side of the Rainbow" into a YouTube search and your target video should come up at the top of the list. Just to confirm that you have the right one, it should clock in at 1:41:36. Time to let the games begin.

Pink Floyd's *Dark Side of the Moon* album begins and ends with the sound of a subtle heartbeat which fades in and fades out. At the risk of giving away some of the good stuff we'll let you know right off the bat that the super cool heartbeat segment which occurs at the end of the album syncs up with Dorothy putting her ear to the Tin Man's chest and listening for a heartbeat.

THE TIMELINE

0:00 ~ In syncing the movie and the album, the opening heartbeat provides a background to the opening credits which seems to convey an appropriate parallel. In both cases, we're just treading water, waiting for the magic to begin.

2:56 ~ As Dorothy attempts to convey her panic about Toto's plight to Auntie Em and Uncle Henry, the viewer is made aware of the conflict over which Dorothy will leave home. In the new soundtrack you hear Pink Floyd singing "But don't leave me."

3:03 ~ As this conversation ends, Dorothy turns and looks around her family's farmland while Pink Floyd is singing "Look around, choose your own ground."

3:19 ~ As Dorothy touches the farmhand Zeke (played by Bert Lahr), you hear "All you touch and all you see."

3:44 ~ The farmhand Hunk (played by Ray Bolger) hits his finger with the hammer during the line "When at last the work is done" and throws the hammer away, symbolizing that his work is done.

4:02 ~ As lifelong Beach Boys fans, this is one of our favorites … as Dorothy balances on a fence with outstretched arms as if she's riding a surf board, the words "Balanced on the biggest wave" are heard in the song "Breathe." Surf's Up!

4:10 ~ Dorothy falls off the fence and is rescued by the farmhands as the chaotic intro to the song "On the Run" begins. Surf's Down!

8:02 ~ This matching transition is so spot-on that for many people it becomes the breakthrough moment forcing the realization that you're onto something special here. Just as Judy Garland's classic rendition of "Somewhere Over the Rainbow" fades out, there is a striking simultaneous convergence. Just as you see Elvira Gulch feverishly pedaling her bicycle, the soundtrack immediately shifts to the jarring sound of blasting chimes and alarms in the song "Time." This example stands out because not only is the timing perfect, the mood of the action and the tone of the music are totally reflective of one another.

10:34 ~ Next we'll take you to the scene where Elvira Gulch has reached the farm and completed her canine confiscation of Toto. Basking in her cruel abduction, she loses track of the basket on the back of her bike where Toto is encaged. Just after a reference to "home", Toto pushes open the lid, hits the ground running, and skedaddles down the road back to Dorothy with, "Waiting for someone or something to show you the way" playing in the background.

11:04 ~ As Dorothy runs away from home the line "No one told you when to run" from the song "Time" is heard.

11:22 ~ During the "Time" guitar solo, the fortune teller sign appears, reading "Past Present and Future."

12:49 ~ As Dorothy enters the fortune teller's trailer, he follows her in and comes up behind her just as the lyrics "Come up behind you again" are heard, again from the song "Time."

13:55 ~ As the fortune teller is convincing Dorothy to go back home, the lyrics "Home, Home again" are heard.

14:50 ~ As Dorothy departs there's another exquisite example of how the song transitions on the album coincide with scene transition in the movie. Just as "The Great Gig in the Sky" kicks in, storm winds kick up foreshadowing the tornado.

15:56 ~ The mellow opening of "Great Gig" suddenly shifts gears with drums, a haunting piano and shrill vocals coinciding with Dorothy almost being hit by a falling tree as the tornado drastically intensifies. The wailing wordless vocals performed by Clare Torry over the next 70 seconds provide a perfect backdrop for the frantic scene as Dorothy finds herself battling the approaching tornado, locked out of the storm cellar, and struggling to make her way back into the house.

17:06 ~ The window sash blows into her bedroom knocking Dorothy out. As she falls onto her bed, those frantic vocals subside and the music takes on a dreamlike tone as Dorothy is seen in a dreamlike trance beginning her transition to Oz.

17:19 ~ As you first see the house spinning upward toward the heavens, "The Great Gig in the Sky" provides the perfectly frenzied musical backdrop.

17:40 ~ When Dorothy wakes up in her now floating house, Clare Torry's powerful vocals begin to build as a terrified Dorothy experiences a series of visions of her family members and the farmhands back home.

18:30 ~ As Dorothy's vision of Elvira Gulch morphs into the Wicked Witch of the West, the operatic vocals resonate like the fuel powering her broomstick as she rides through the tornado.

19:31 ~ One extremely effective technique employed in the cinematography of *The Wizard of Oz* was the use of black & white sepia film for all the "Kansas footage" which bookends the film, and the beautiful Technicolor film for all of the "Oz footage."

So, this point in the film is always a breathtaking one and it is also certainly a pinnacle in the *Dark Side of the Rainbow* concept providing yet another example of where a shift in the movie scene coincides in dramatic perfection with a new song starting on the album. This transition is absolutely spot-on perfect.

After the spinning house has crash landed, Dorothy gets up and cautiously makes her way toward the door. As she tentatively opens it, upon the first glimpse of color in the film you hear the first cash register "ka-ching" the opening note of the song "Money." For the record, no pun intended, "Money" was the only hit single from the album, peaking at #13 in 1972.

21:08 ~ Glinda, the Good Witch of the North, pops up on the horizon in her little magical bubble ride. As the bubble of the Good Witch floats toward Dorothy and Toto you hear the line, "Don't give me that do-goody-good bullshit."

25:00 ~ The munchkins' dance seems to be perfectly choreographed to "Money."

27:36 ~ In another example of movie action syncing with song beginnings, the munchkin ballerinas part the line of soldiers and make their entrance just as the first words of "Us and Them" are heard.

28:06 ~ Following the ballerinas, the Lollipop Guild munchkins amble onto center stage and the camera zooms in on them as the vocals to "Us and Them" start again. The jerky style of their dancing and singing matches the music in a bizarrely appealing fashion.

28:44 ~ At exactly the time the "Forward he cried" lyric is heard, Dorothy turns to face forward.

29:10 ~ Exactly when the black-cloaked Wicked Witch of the West comes into full view, the words "Black, black, black" are heard. The next lyrics heard are "And blue, blue, blue," so as the black and blue lines are heard from Pink Floyd the action in the film depicts an exchange between the witch dressed in black and Dorothy dressed in blue.

29:26 – There is only a small segment of the film when there are actually three witches in play at the same time. The Good Witch of the North looks on as the Wicked Witch of the West goes over to confirm the demise of her sister the Wicked Witch of the East, who is lying dead underneath Dorothy's house. The lyrics heard at this point are "… and who knows which is which and who is who."

29:43 – After the Wicked Witch of the West ascends the ramp to confront Dorothy and Glinda, the words "Up, Up, Up" are heard.

29:49 – As she descends the ramp the words "Down, Down, Down" are heard. For these last two segments, this second one is actually the more compelling for the following reason. When you hear the "Up's" the witch is already at the top of the ramp; when you hear the "Down's" she is actually in the process of descending as if she's following directions given to her by the music.

29:58 – As you no doubt recall, the only portion of the dead witch's body which is visible are her feet, which extend out from under the house. Right after her feet shrivel and disappear under the house, you hear the words "And in the end."

30:31 – The Wicked Witch of the West's hand seems to form a gun and point at Dorothy to the lyrics "Said the man with the gun."

32:20 – Here's another one where the timing couldn't get any more precise. Just as Glinda reenters her magic bubble to depart, you hear the words "Out, Out, Out."

33:47 – Occurring next is another example of scene-change perfectly matching song-change. Just as Dorothy has finished waving goodbye to the munchkins, the scene shifts to her and Toto traversing the Yellow Brick Road. At precisely the same moment "Us and Them" fades out, giving way to "Any Color You Like."

37:12 – As the song "Brain Damage" begins, the scarecrow is singing "If I Only Had a Brain."

37:47 ~ During "Brain Damage" as Dorothy and the scarecrow are on the Yellow Brick Road you hear the words "Got to keep the loonies on the path."

42:40 ~ The album ends as it begins, with a heartbeat. As the heartbeat fades away, Dorothy puts her ear to the tin man's chest listening for the heartbeat that isn't there.

DECISION TIME ~ Alright class, now that you've experienced the *Dark Side of the Rainbow* phenomenon, what do you think? Coincidence or collusion? On one hand, aren't there almost too many coincidences for this not to have been some kind of conscious plan?

But Pink Floyd has always adamantly denied any connection whatsoever. "It's unthinkable that we would have felt that it was really important to work with Judy Garland," Pink Floyd drummer Nick Mason told MTV in 1997. "It's absolute nonsense. It has nothing to do with *The Wizard of Oz*," Mason said before facetiously adding, "It was all based on *The Sound of Music*."

The album's engineer, Alan Parsons, when asked if the parallels between the movie and the album were intentional, also denied it. "There simply wasn't the mechanics to do it," he said. "We had no means of playing videotapes in the room at all. I don't think VHS had come along by '72, had it?"

However, in assessing Parsons' quote, it almost makes us **more** suspicious than less. True, there was no home video when the album was recorded in 1972, but we're talking Pink Floyd here. Certainly they had the money to make the video accessible had it been their desire. There wasn't home video, but professional video had existed for decades and obviously this would have been within their means both financially and logistically.

BOTH SIDES NOW ~ In our attempt to present all the pertinent information on both sides of the debate, allow us to offer the three following arguments which would support the belief that this was not something Pink Floyd did on purpose.

#1) ANIMOSITY ~ Especially during the band's later years, the members of Pink Floyd did not get along. In particular Roger Waters and David Gilmore, essentially the band's leaders, were at extreme odds with one another and the bickering and lawsuits that characterized this relationship could make for an article in and of itself. The level of animosity that existed would seem so significant that it would be difficult for everyone involved to just jointly sit on such a sophisticated secret like one big happy family.

#2) CONSPIRACY ~ The recording process to make an album involves more people than just the band. You've got a producer, a sound engineer, and who knows how many others. Whatever that number of "others" might be, anyway you cut it, there is a whole second tier of conspirators who would be capable of letting the cat out of the bag. That's a lot of people to keep quiet for a long time.

#3) TIMING ~ If Pink Floyd planned the whole *Dark Side of the Rainbow* concept, they would have had to channel a tremendous amount of creative time and energy. If such an effort had been put forth, it doesn't seem like they would have wanted to wait so long to enjoy the public reaction to what they had done. The first documented mention of the phenomenon did not occur until 1995.

You'd think that if they'd really done this, the plan would have involved "leaking" the story to the public without waiting 23 years to do it. After the leak, there could have been a plan to play coy and pretend it was all a coincidence but if there was a game afoot, why wait over two decades to let the game begin?

Obviously, possible death-bed confessions notwithstanding, whether or not Pink Floyd intentionally synced *Dark Side of the Moon* to *The Wizard of Oz* is something we'll probably never know with 100% certainty. There's compelling evidence which certainly serpentines.

While we shared an element of logic which would seem to give the disbelievers an easy out, we are hereby choosing to throw the whole element of question up for grabs. We've just taken our magnifying glass back to Pink Floyd's 1995 album *Pulse* and uncovered the following subtle nuances. If you look closely in the iris of the eye you can make out hidden images of an old bicycle (like Elvira's) and a pair of red shoes (like Dorothy's).

The album came out in May of that year and the first public discussions of the synchronicities did not occur until August. At the very least this would seem to arouse suspicion that the album cover was a Floyd boys' ploy to nudge the world into stumbling upon the media manipulation they had orchestrated decades before.

In the history of music, no album has ever stayed on the charts for longer than Pink Floyd's *Dark Side of the Moon* and in the history of movies, no film has ever stayed in the hearts of the public longer than *The Wizard of Oz*. Subsequently the synchronicity is certainly sound, no pun intended.

MELANIE'S HAPPY HIPPIE CHRISTMAS GIFT

FLASH FROM THE PAST ~ One of the oldest surviving pictures of us was taken in Tim's backyard during our junior year in high school. We are sitting in a couple of those old-fashioned aluminum webbed chairs with a gatefold vinyl record album opened on our laps. The album was *Candles in the Rain* by Melanie and that song was about her breakthrough performance at Woodstock in 1969. Over the past few years, we've actually been able to cultivate a bit of a friendship with Melanie. It's a story that involves everything from tequila shots, to mistaken identities, to a painted Christmas rock.

Here's her long-story-short bio. After Melanie's Woodstock breakthrough, she carved out a successful career selling more records than any female artist in the world in 1972, and becoming the first female solo artist to ever have three songs in the Top 40 at the same time. Not a bad resumé by anyone's standards. If you want one go-to song that would make you say, "Oh yeah, I remember her," go to YouTube and punch in "Brand New Key" by Melanie.

The Melanie album that we are holding in the picture on the back cover of this book was the first album we ever bought together as a couple, pooling our money to do so late in our freshman year in high school. She was always one of our favorite artists and our album collection eventually expanded to 18.

When we find out that she is going to be playing at the Rochester Institute of Technology in May of 2017 it clearly becomes a must-see event for us. As we prepare to see Melanie's concert in Rochester, we're looking at our vintage photo from 1971 and we get the quirky idea to try and recreate our 1971 pose in 2017. Our results are successful enough that we come up with a plan to take our then-and-now pictures to the show and see if we can come up with a way to get an "in" with the artist. At this point you can look at the back cover of this book to see the pictures we just described.

We arrive at the venue early and notice Melanie's son Beau, who is also her lead guitarist, on stage setting up their equipment. We're sure most people don't realize who he is and we subtly and politely approach the stage and wait for an auspicious moment to engage him, and show him our picture.

When he notices us, we tell him that we have something we'd like to have him see and we share our picture. "That's awesome," Beau says, clearly impressed with our then-and-now photo, "Mom will definitely enjoy seeing this."

In order to understand this next part of our story we need to fill you in on the physical layout of this venue. The building is rectangular in shape and the stage is nestled back in one corner. The "backstage" area where the performers wait to make their entrance is in the opposite corner of the building.

Odd set up, but the reality of the situation is that this establishment is primarily a large bar/restaurant. At any rate, when performers are introduced, they usually emerge from the back corner, and make their way through the crowd to the stage.

Melanie's son Beau explains to us that her entrance is going to be different. Rather than have her tread through the entire crowd, they're going to walk her around the outside of the building and have her enter through an emergency exit door just beside the stage. The building is all glass on that side and Beau says, "When you notice us approaching come to the door, they'll let you out, and you can show Mom your picture."

So, our photographic efforts are enough to earn us a brief audience with Melanie before the concert at RIT. As we will convey more thoroughly throughout this chapter, her quirky hippie chick shtick still clicks. After admiring our pictures, she leaves us saying, "Please send me that picture for Christmas." Okay, we're thinking, but this RIT concert is in May.

We would love to tell you that our master plan at the time of the original picture was to enable us to recreate that pose 45 years later in order to endear ourselves to Melanie. But to use the title of one of her songs, even the most gullible of the "Beautiful People" in our audience are not going to buy that, which makes all of you as smart as you are beautiful.

But that May we make a mental note of it and in December, we double down on our dedication and stage a second photo op with us surrounded by the 18 Melanie albums we still have in our collection. We send that, along with our then-and-now pic, to Melanie during the week before Christmas. We are thrilled to receive a personal response back from her, the first of what would become many. We'll share a few of them with you as they convey how far out there our classic hippie friend can be.

Her response to the pic was, "Love the web aluminum chairs! You look the same! Congratulations on being together! Where is the cat? Love, Melanie." To this day we have no idea what she means about the cat. There's no cat in either picture. But we're so happy just to be corresponding with her that we choose not to bring it up.

KEEP THE BALL ROLLIN' ~ So at that point we're contemplating our next move just to try to keep the channel of communications open with her. We ask ourselves, "What in the world could we give her as some type of Christmas gift that might spark the continuance of the correspondence thread?" It occurs to us that perhaps we could entertain her with some of our writing and with the seasonal theme in mind, we send her a piece we had written in 2017 on Christmas Island.

This turns out to be a fortuitously prophetic move on our part. Melanie writes back saying, "Your writing is beautiful. What you wrote about me before maybe we could include it in my newsletter? A photo too if you have one. How about the ones with my album?"

As we sit in front of our keyboard on the Saturday night before Christmas that December, volleying emails back and forth with Melanie, it is really a "pinch me" moment.

We tell her that we would be honored to write our Melanie story for her newsletter and proud to have our photo shoot included in her online material. Melanie writes back and explains to us that her newsletter is published bi-monthly and her next edition will come out in February.

HIPPIE RANTS ~ We wanted to be selective in deciding which of her hippie rants to include and this next one is our very favorite. In italics below is our pep talk, delivered by Melanie, in which she strives to inspire us as we write for her February 2018 newsletter.

Well, you know what is coming next? If there was to be a Melanie month, it would be February. The red month. Hearts, flowers and chocolate. The Valentine month and my birthday. Time for a pagan celebration dancing in the moonlight around a drum circle, around a fire, sparks flying in my mind. I'm going to fast in January to prepare, right after the champagne. January 2, third, or maybe the fifth. Juice cleanse and the deep breathing. I will reunite with the rhythm of the wind and water.

Melanie's comments above leave one question unanswered. We have no idea why January 4 is off the table as an option for the beginning of the fast. That will have to remain yet another meandering Melanie mystery.

The next Melanie email is first opened by Tim and it sparks an idea. The point of view for the next part of our story needs to shift from first person "combined" to first person "singular." Tim, alone, will tell the tale for the next few paragraphs.

HI, IT'S TIM ~ Okay, now that Deb has left the room, I'll tell you how this next part goes down. Melanie's email shares the very happy hippie message that she's just finished her painting of Christmas rocks which are to be her gifts for family and friends.

Unbeknownst to Deb, I send Melanie an email asking if there is any way I could bless Deb with a hand-painted Christmas rock personalized to us and signed by her.

Here is the part where Melanie truly becomes a Christmas angel. She stays up until 3:00 in the morning painting a rock for Deb, and has to overnight it the next morning for the stone to get here in time for Christmas.

TO ALL A GOOD NIGHT ~ An added level of drama ensues on Christmas Eve when the tracking number shows the package as having been delivered, but it is nowhere in sight. Just as the panic mode is about to set in, our neighbor knocks on the door and hands off the precious parcel which had inadvertently been delivered next door. She certainly would have brought it over earlier had she only known it was the virtual Rosetta Stone she had signed for.

When the delivery confirmation reaches Melanie, she writes, "Tim, in the newsletter will you tell the story of the surprise package delivery and how I tried to be too much like an adult by insuring it. I could tell it but I would probably fudge up the story a bit you know, but everything I make up is true :) Love, Melanie"

MIDSUMMER TRILOGY ~ In August of 2018 we enjoyed a 3-day musical experience we wrote about in a series we called *A Midsummer Night Trilogy*. This concert trifecta consisted of

- Almost Queen in Rochester
- The Beach Boys in Canandaigua
- Melanie in Buffalo

Almost Queen is considered to be the hands-down best Queen cover band and arguably the best cover band out there, period. Despite their talent, there's not a lot of story to tell about the band because obviously you know exactly what you'll be getting. This concert did have a VIP package that we have never seen exactly replicated at any show we have attended.

For an extra $30 each we receive a package of food/souvenir perks and most importantly a yellow wristband entitling us to "front stage access." There is an area about 20 feet square, in front of the left half of the stage, which is cordoned off and tightly guarded by our crack VIP enforcement team. This is an outdoor general admission venue which is part of a "Party in the Park" summer concert series offered by the city of Rochester. The people who aren't "very important" only pay $5 to get in so the park is packed and it is nice to be able to circumvent the crowd and walk right up close to the stage.

After starting with Queen and ending with Melanie, in between we revved up the hot rods, rode the waves, and felt the good vibrations with the Beach Boys. We detailed our connection with "America's Band" earlier in this chapter so we will consider them covered.

Returning to the Melanie thread ... when we see that she is playing in Buffalo, there is no question that we will be there. At this point we are going to throw out a little teaser and share with you the prospect that this concert story will absolutely become our best and most bizarre of all-time. It even has an element of alchemy where we are going to turn 5¢ into $500. You'll definitely want to stick around for that feat.

Our use of the word "prospect" in the previous paragraph was calculated, alluding to the concept of prospecting for gold. Just so nobody's putting this book down to reach for a dictionary, alchemy is the medieval belief that base metals, usually lead, could be turned into gold.

Melanie is playing at a club called AcQua which is a nice venue sitting right on the Niagara River. The doors open at 6:00 with the show starting at 8:00. We arrive a little before 6:00 hoping to secure a good spot, and we have brought our aforementioned then-and-now picture and the original 1971 album (which we are holding in the picture) hoping to get them signed.

We are amongst the first people there and when we get to the stage area the very front row of tables are marked "reserved," but we are able to secure a great spot in the second row with a direct line of vision only about 15 feet away from where Melanie will be performing.

ESTABLISHING A RECONNECTION ~ After settling in at our table we notice Melanie's son Beau, once again setting up the equipment. We walk up to say hi and he does recognize us from our picture being on their website. Deb tells him that we are hoping to have his Mom sign our picture and album and she wonders if he can take our pieces backstage and have her sign them because we don't want to bother her in person.

Beau explains that his mother is not there yet, but he looks at us and says, "Oh, my Mom is going to want to talk to you after the show and you'll have the opportunity to get everything signed."

So that all seems great, but we're a little confused as to how the logistics of this are all going to work out. Is he going to come out and look for us after the show? It all sounds a little sketchy, and we'll share with you that at this stage of our story there is a misconception in the equation here which will not be fully revealed until the very end of the evening.

But at this point, let's get on with the show. That majestic Melanie voice is still magical and her son Beau is an absolutely awesome lead guitarist. The setting is perfect and, in the background as she performs, we watch the shimmering sun serenely set on the shoreline behind her. The sky turns into a palette of pretty pink and purple pastels and the sun reflects a rainbow of colors across the wavy waters of the rippling river.

BACK TO THE SHOW ~ About a third of the way through the show Melanie starts to drink a cup of tea which has been set on the table beside her. After her first sip she immediately says, "You know what I need? I need some hot water with lemon juice. Can somebody get me that?" A lady sitting right in front of us, who is clearly part of the Melanie entourage, immediately leaves and soon returns with her hot beverage.

Continuing on the subject of beverages, about halfway through the show Melanie does exactly the same thing we saw her do at RIT. She sweetly and directly announces to the crowd that at this point in her show she likes to start sipping on a glass of tequila which has been placed on the table to her right. She removes the napkin that has been covering the glass, picks it up, and says, "This is gold tequila. I need clear tequila. Could somebody get me a glass of clear tequila?"

TEQUILA SUNRISE ~ Noticing that after a few more songs Melanie's tequila has not yet been delivered, Deb leans forward toward the lady who had procured her previous drink and asks, "Melanie still doesn't have her tequila; would you like me to go get it for her?" Clearly busy on her phone doing something, the lady signals the go-ahead for Deb to get the tequila. Usually stories with Deb on the prowl for tequila do not end well but this one does come with a happy ending.

Deb gets up, goes to the bar and retrieves the tequila. After waiting for Melanie to finish her song, Deb walks up to her, places her drink on the table and turns to walk back to her seat. After two steps, Deb is halted by Melanie's request to come back and accept accolades for the beautifully flowered hippie-style dress she is wearing. Deb pauses when Melanie says, "Oh, I love your dress. Are you a server? Do all the servers wear those pretty flowered dresses?" What follows next is a 90-second conversation between Deb and Melanie which is broadcast live to everyone at the venue because the whole thing is taking place right by Melanie's microphone.

Truth be told, Deb would never have been presumptuous enough to try and initiate a conversation with Melanie in this scenario, but inadvertently provided with an in by Melanie herself, Deb becomes a force to be reckoned with. She spins around, returns to the stage, and says, "Thank you for liking my dress. You might remember us as the couple whose picture you put on your website and you painted a personalized rock for us last Christmas."

REMEMBER US ~ Then Melanie's son Beau chimes in reminding her, "Mom, they're the couple who wrote the article about you. You're going to be talking to them after the show tonight." At this point all the dots are connecting in Melanie's hippie brain and she says, "Oh yes, now I remember who you are."

Keep in mind this conversation is taking place right by Melanie's microphone so everyone in the venue is hearing every word. For about 90 seconds that night the entire crowd is being entertained by the "Deb & Melanie Show." A true meeting of the minds.

Let us share with you one other unusual thread of activity running through this enchanted evening. As we sit on the fringe of the most hardcore Melanie fans within driving distance, one guy leans over and says to us, "You know, with your wristbands you get two free drinks each." Right off the bat this makes no sense to us because we're thinking that we spent $42 each for these tickets and they are about to bring us $36 worth of free drinks. The explanation for this, as well as the night's other mysteries, only becomes clear to us in the final chapter of this story. Read on.

AUTOGRAPH ANXIETY ~ Deb's conversation with Melanie and Beau serves to reinforce our hope that we will achieve our goal of having her sign our souvenirs, but we're still concerned that the process by which this will come to fruition has not been specifically defined at all. When the show ends, we walk from the outdoor concert venue back into the lobby and try to figure things out. We're thinking we might see Beau, but that doesn't happen.

At this point we look for somebody on the staff and ask, "If we're supposed to get something signed by Melanie after the show, where do we go?" They point us toward a door at the side of the lobby where two men are standing. As we approach, we hear one of the men saying something about wristbands which we can't precisely make out. As we get closer, the second man says, "That's the lady who was right up on stage with her. They're okay."

SOLVING THE MYSTERIES ~ We walk into the side room and only gradually are the details of what has actually happened this night revealed to us. Just to review, here is our mystery list:

1 - Why does Beau, when we talk to him during set-up, nonchalantly tell us that his mother will look forward to talking to us after the show and repeat the premise when Deb is at the stage?

2 – Why do our $42 tickets warrant $36 worth of free wine?

3 – What was the conversation the two men at the door had about our wristbands?

We will eventually get around to solving these mysteries but let's return to where we left off and continue the story. We walk into this side room to find about 15 people and one of the most luxurious buffet spreads we have ever seen.

The occupants of the room are clearly the inner realm of the Melanie world. Most are toting Melanie memorabilia and as we discreetly listen in on the conversations surrounding us, these people know their stuff. They have clearly been reading and reflecting upon her lyrics for as long as we have.

WRISTBAND REVELATIONS ~ Then through a combination of observation and conversation in Melanie nation, another realization begins to dawn upon us. Everyone in the room is wearing the solid orange wristband that we also have on, which was needed to get from the restaurant to the concert area of the venue.

The "observation" component from the first sentence of the previous paragraph is that we notice everyone else in the room is also sporting a solid yellow wristband. The "conversation" component is that we begin to hear people talking about the $250 they each paid for this "Meet and Greet."

So, at this point we are finally going to connect the dots for you regarding us being alchemists who could turn two 5¢ wristbands into $500. We finally realize that each of these people has paid $250 apiece to gain entry into this Meet and Greet that we have just casually and innocently strolled into.

By perhaps the quirkiest example of fate that has occurred to us in our concert careers, the VIP yellow wristbands we had been given at the Almost Queen concert in Rochester two nights earlier are close enough to the yellow AcQua wristbands that at a casual glimpse they manage to pass for $250 Melanie wristbands throughout the night. The answers to all three questions we posed above are provided to us at this moment.

1 - The reason Beau assumed we would be in this room to get autographs is because he saw the yellow wristbands.

2 - The reason the waitress brought us $36 worth of free wine was because she saw the yellow wristbands.

3 - And the element of hesitancy on the part of one of the two door guards was that he noticed that our yellow wristbands seemed to be a little different than the others.

PARTY CRASHERS ~ Subsequently, we do realize that we are not actually supposed to be at this $250-per-person Melanie "Meet and Greet" but we can honestly say that we were personally invited by her son Beau who happens to walk in at that moment and engage us in conversation. He enjoys hearing our stories about which of his mother's songs meant the most to us and why, which gives us cause to realize we are where we are supposed to be.

Beau announces that his Mom will be down in about 15 minutes. This announcement prompts most in the room to line up at the buffet, but in all honesty, we are just too excited to eat. The first time we met Melanie, our then-and-now picture and conversation with her son had enabled us to enjoy a brief audience with her. This time we know we will have a few minutes with her and be able to have her sign the picture and album we've cherished since 1971.

MEETING MELANIE ~ Eventually Melanie enters the room and her anxious assembly of ardent supporters politely form a line. As Melanie is seated at her signing table, each group gathers around to share a few moments with this musical legend. As we patiently wait our turn, we are more confident than nervous.

Nobody else in this room has their picture on her website. Nobody else in this room received a painted rock from her last Christmas. We are about to enjoy conversation, an autograph session and a photo op with the musical artist for whom we pooled our money to buy the very first album we ever bought as a couple.

It's almost hard to put into words how much this one meant to us. When we got back to our hotel, we were literally pinching ourselves and asking each other, "Did this really happen tonight?"

CHAPTER 11
ON THE HOMEFRONT

LEGAL EAGLE SHELDON BOYCE

A good friend of ours, Sheldon Boyce, is an attorney and also the judge here in town. Every Sunday from 8:00 to 9:00 am, Sheldon co-hosts a show on a local radio station which answers legal questions for free on a call-in basis. Sheldon enjoys the opportunity to give back to the community and as he says, "There is nothing like live radio."

Playing upon that premise, he shared with us some highlights from the past several years of the show. Here are our two favorites respectively titled "The Dentist" and "The Doper."

SUCK IT UP ~ One morning they get a call from a woman who wants to know if she has a claim for dental malpractice. Due to her recent dental work, she speaks with a lisp. When prompted for the details it sounds like she says, "The dentist fucked up my tooth."

There was no tape delay broadcast equipment in play. The water's under the bridge at this point, so all Sheldon can do is frantically signal the producer to disconnect the caller and apologize to the audience for the foul language.

The cherry on top that absolutely makes this story is that the lady subsequently calls the producer back to tell him that what she had actually said was, "The dentist sucked up my tooth" (meaning with his dental suction device). If it had been a TV show this incident might have been a nominee for all-time *Wheel of Fortune* bloopers.

HIGH TIMES ~ Next, let's light up the topic of legalization of marijuana. And you can't help but love the irony of this one; we're not sure if this was done specifically in his honor, but on the occasion of Tim's birthday on January 28, 2018, the radio show hit the airwaves with a special edition devoted to the legalization of marijuana.

On this show they receive a call from Rick, a guy who tells it like it is. He shares that in his personal experience, when he smokes pot and takes to the road, he is a terrible driver. Therefore, he is against the legalization of marijuana. He goes on to say that after he smokes, his driving is compromised for two days.

We subsequently come to two conclusions about Rick. We don't think anybody's going to be rushing to ask him for a ride anywhere soon. On the other hand, we're thinking there may be many people wondering where he gets his pot. That weed that lasts for two days is pretty tough to find.

MARY THERESE ~ OUR MISS U.S.A. NEIGHBOR

Our home has an unusual setup which we need to explain in order for this next story to completely come together. We are only four doors from the four corners of the little town of Mendon, NY. We are on the edge of the business district of town which is by no means expansive. Our property is the last one to have commercial zoning and for over a century it served as a combination of residence and business for a variety of owners.

When we bought it, we turned the business half of the building into part of our living quarters, which has some slightly unusual ramifications. Right now, as we sit at our computers, the 25-foot span in front of us is mostly glass and the edge of the road is only twenty feet away. It's a bit like living in a fish bowl but we enjoy watching the world go by and from a writer's perspective it adds the benefit that sometimes rather than us having to find stories, the stories find us. For example…

STRANGER DANGER ~ Last St. Patrick's Day we are working on an article, being careful not to let any green beer spill onto our workspace, when we notice a man walk by the front of our house one way and then seconds later cross back. At that point, our curiosity aroused, we walk to the front door to take a closer look. It is an elderly man dressed only in a bath robe, holding a catheter bag, and looking clearly lost and confused.

After getting him inside our house to assist him in troubleshooting the situation, he asks us, "Do you know where Miss America is?" So, let's summarize things at this point. In our house right now we have an old guy that we don't know, wearing only a bathrobe with a catheter bag, and inquiring as to the whereabouts of Miss America.

For most folks, this might present as a scenario almost too bizarre to be true. But for us, it just comes with the territory in our neighborhood and we are actually able to connect the dots quite quickly. In a comment that not many people could say, we have an assisted living senior center three doors down from us and "Miss America" lives just around the corner.

The senior center is self-explanatory, and our surprise guest had wandered off from there, but we need to address the mention of Miss America. We will revert to an alternate title at this point and explain that actually Miss USA lives right around the corner from us in beautiful downtown Mendon.

MISS USA ~ Our good friend, and occasional partner in crime, Mary Therese Friel, won the Miss USA Pageant in 1979. Before we share some stories about our collaborations with Mary Therese and her husband Kent, please allow us to explain the pageantry parlance pertaining to the alternate titles. Separate contests, the Miss USA winner goes on to compete in the Miss Universe pageant while Miss America has no follow up event.

Mary Therese finished sixth in the Miss Universe pageant which was held in Perth, Australia that year, and to us she'll always be #1. In addition to running the MTF Modeling Agency, Mary Therese and Kent are involved in so many philanthropic community causes it's difficult to keep track of them all. Honest to God, as we sat here typing this, they just popped up on our local TV news in a spot assisting the animal shelter to find adoptive homes for abandoned pets. They've become local celebrities.

At this point we need to connect one more dot for you. If you're following this closely one question still remaining should be, "How does catheter-man know Miss America?" The answer to this not only connects the final dot, it provides yet another example of the altruism of Mary Therese and Kent. We have seen them on the porch of the senior center volunteering their time to facilitate interaction between therapy dogs and the seniors at the center.

If for any reason you're curious about what we sound like in person you could actually hear us in archived airings of the Mary Therese and Kent Friel radio show *ROC Image Radio*. Google WAYO 104.3 FM and the name of that show and you will see a chronological listing of all their programs. We were their guests on 02.25.2020, 10.29.2019 and 02.06.2018.

Here's one funny story that they recently shared with us. One day, out of the blue, Mary Therese gets a call from a friend of hers who says, "Oh my God, did you know that you're in the Tom Cruise movie that just came out on video?" Mary Therese has no idea what she is talking about and here's the explanation for why.

MOVIE MADNESS ~ In the opening sequence of the film *American Made*, the director establishes the time setting by using a compilation of iconic video snippets from 1979. One of the snippets used is Mary Therese enjoying her crowning moment and traditional walk as the new Miss USA. An irony in how this story plays out is that Mary Therese was never told that she would appear in the movie. The rights to the video footage are owned by the pageant, so they are not obligated to share release information with any of the contestants, nor are there any royalties. In this case, the check is **not** in the mail.

When we are talking to Mary Therese and Kent about this, they share with us the fact that they, on a few occasions, had actually planned on going to see that movie at the theater when it was released. However, for various reasons, things never worked out. How funny would that have been if they'd gone? Imagine yourself settling into your comfy movie seat to enjoy the latest Tom Cruise movie and you actually appear in the film before he does!

Mary Therese was very animated as she described what her hypothetical reaction to the above scenario might have been. Would she have been calm, cool, and collected? Not likely. That's Kent's job. She would have put her hands to her face, leaned over and excitedly whispered, "Oh my gosh, Kent, is that me? Is it really me?" When you're a former Miss USA, these things can happen.

THE HIPPIES, THE HOODS AND THE JOCKS

Our book contains just one story from our high school days but it is a good one which is at or near the top of the list of our articles for which we received the greatest amount of feedback. We grew up in Honeoye Falls and Lima, two small towns in Upstate New York, and probably never would have known each other were it not for a quirky event that took place in between our 8th and 9th grade years. The towns that we lived in voted to merge the two separate school districts into one.

HF-L MERGER ~ So we were the first class to spend all four of our high school years in this newly formed district and, under those circumstances, there were some highly historical and humorous experiences to be explored. When two separate high schools combine into one, some issues arise that might not immediately occur to you.

With the vote approving the merger not occurring until June 12th, there was a lot that had to be done, and not much time in which to do it. One particularly tricky aspect of this was sports. All the HF-L teams took the field that fall in the already existing uniforms of either Lima or Honeoye Falls.

And before any new uniforms could even be ordered, there were the questions of what would be the newly formed district's mascot and colors. Lima's nickname was the Indians, and they wore purple and gold. Honeoye Falls was the Hornets, who wore orange and black.

The decision was made that the student body would get to vote, and we were given two choices. So as to avoid any appearance of favoritism, the four previous colors of the two schools were offered in new combinations. Our two choices were that we could become the black and gold "Cougars" or the purple and orange "Sunrisers." Which of course led to the obvious question of, "What the hell is a Sunriser?"

HIGH SCHOOL CLIQUES ~ Ironically, the various existing high school cliques factored significantly into the balloting process. This might be generalizing a bit, but there was a solid underlying truth. The three dominant high school cliques at the time were the Jocks, the Hippies, and the Hoods. The Jocks, of course, were the kids who played sports. The Hippies and the Hoods shared the commonality that they were non-athletes but other than that, they were different breeds of cats.

The quickest means of identification was to get a look at the artwork on their spiral 3-ring binders. If it was colorful and flowery, you were looking at a Hippie. If it had dark, skull and crossbones imagery, you were looking at a Hood. Hoods smoked cigarettes. Hippies smoked something else. Hippies could watch *The Brady Bunch* and *The Partridge Family* on TV. Hoods could not.

Hippies operated on a "Peace, Love, Woodstock" vibe. Hoods often had anger management issues. Subsequently the Hoods fought a lot, but the Hippies didn't.

UNLIKELY COALITION ~ At any rate, as this whole school colors and mascot debate was consuming the student body, the Hippies and the Hoods formed an unlikely coalition. The two groups coalesced to rally around the Sunrisers/Purple & Orange nickname/color scheme option, but of course for totally different reasons.

The Hoods for the most part hated the Jocks and they thought it would be embarrassing for the school teams to have to take the field in those colors. The Hippies thought the funky Purple & Orange color scheme would be "Far Out and Groovy."

We Jocks were pretty solidly behind the Cougar/Black & Gold option, which seemed like the inevitable choice but the whole Hippie/Hood coalition was just bizarre enough to add an air of tension to the entire process. Why should they get to vote when they were never going to wear the uniforms? But democracy prevailed and so did Cougar Black & Gold.

ASSESSING THE OUTCOME ~ As the Jocks breathed a sigh of relief in the locker rooms the afternoon after the results were announced, there were prevailing theories and jokes as to what led to the final vote tally. The Hippies had all gotten high and forgotten it was Election Day. The Hoods had forgotten it was Election Day and skipped school.

One irony about the Purple & Orange "Sunriser" coalition of Hoods and Hippies was that getting up early was not a strong suit for either group. Maybe they all just slept in and didn't make it to the ballot box.

Here is a final thought on the jokes and theories surrounding the new nickname, and this might have been the only thing that the Jocks, Hippies and Hoods all agreed on. The humorous take on things was that if we were going to combine the old colors from each school, we should also find a way to combine the old mascots as well.

MASCOT WITH MAXIMUM MARKETABILITY ~ And one choice clearly emerged as the student favorite. How about we take Indians (from Lima) and Hornets (from Honeoye Falls) and come up with the clever combination of the HF-L Horny Indians? It wouldn't have scored high on the scale of political correctness, but think of the merchandise we could have sold! And wouldn't an air of frivolity have been added to the Art Club's task of designing the new logo?

SKYLER SMITH'S TOUR OF MENDON

If we had to pick one component of our writing that has been the most rewarding, it would be the concept which we will address in this chapter. We have a special needs son named Skyler and although he does have developmental delays across the board, he oozes charisma and has a great capacity for happiness.

He always enjoyed writing stories and his vivid imagination has contributed to some creative material. We always considered this a blessing as it provided an opportunity for us to work with him on his writing skills using material that he had personally generated. On many occasions the two of us would be collaborating on our newest feature and he would set up shop right next to us and begin to write one of his stories.

We were awash with parenting perfection as we joyfully modeled intellectual endeavors which he attempted to emulate. Then one day he came to us and said, "I'm working on an article for the paper and I'd like you to let them know I'll have it done by the weekend."

This turn of events obviously created a bit of a dilemma for us. While we always encouraged his writing, frankly stated, the material he generated wasn't going to make it into the paper. So we started thinking … thinking … thinking … what could an approach be whereby Skyler would be a genuine participant in a three-way writing collaboration that could actually end up in the paper?

The lightning bolt emanating from our brainstorm was "Skyler Smith's Tour of Mendon." This bolt of brilliance turned out to be quadrilaterally symbiotic. Sometimes we just make up expressions, which we admittedly may have just done at the end of that previous sentence. But we promise to make sense of that "quadrilaterally symbiotic" term in an upcoming paragraph.

Part of what made the concept so successful was that it was always written through Skyler's point of view. That concept actually opened up some avenues of creative literary opportunity in our writing. When you are viewing the world through the eyes of a child, you are afforded opportunities to address your subject matter with an air of innocent naiveté which would not be possible if you were writing from a truly adult perspective.

Returning to that term of quadrilaterally symbiotic which we kind of made up, the concept benefitted so many people it was remarkable. We broke it down in four basic categories as follows. The local businesses benefitted from the exposure. The community in general was entertained which in turn generated more readers for the newspaper. And finally, Skyler's self-confidence was boosted as he became a semi-celebrity in town. So, there's your quadrilaterally symbiotic; feel free to use it any time.

So how 'bout we get this tour on the road? Skyler's series was originally conceived to run just a couple of weeks but the damn thing got so popular in town it was held over for almost two years. We decided that 100 weeks would be a nice round number and we determined to have weeks 96-100 be comprised by what we might call "Skyler's Greatest Hits." So right now, take it away Skyler!

IT'S WEEK 96, I BEGIN MY LAST LICKS

HIATUS AT A HUNDRED ~ This is Skyler Smith coming to my readers with an important announcement. After a wonderful run of almost two years now, I have decided to pick my 100th column to become a milestone piece which will be titled "Hiatus at a Hundred." After that I'm going to hit the pause button on my column, step back, and take a break.

I'm sure some of you will be taking this pretty hard, but do know that I plan to provide counseling during your period of grieving and help you masterfully manage your melancholy. We are going to have some fun before I go as I'll be taking you on a stroll down Memory Lane these next few weeks as I share with you highlights of my most well-received installments.

Furthermore, let it be known that I will be back; you can count on that. Notice my choice of words, I said, "hiatus" as opposed to "retirement." No siree, even after my initial run comes to a pause, you will not have heard the last of Skyler Smith. It's probably appropriate that at this point I lead into this storyline by sharing with you the background on how this whole crazy thing got started.

THE BACKSTORY ~ Back in the spring of 2017, as I was nearing the completion of my junior year at HF-L, I remember watching Deb and Dad work on their articles for the *Sentinel*. They always seemed to be having so much fun that it made me want a piece of the action.

So, I went to them with the proclamation that, "I want to write for the *Sentinel* too." At that point our collective wheels began to spin with the operative question being, "What would be a concept that the three of us could collaborate on which would also be good for the community and good for the *Sentinel*?"

The answer to that question was the birth of my column "Skyler Smith's Tour of Mendon."

That summer we began to approach some local business people we knew and ask if they would like to have us tell their stories. Our approach became quite uniform. We would generate a list of questions which we would supply to the interviewees ahead of time so they could give some thought to their answers and be more comfortable during the actual interview.

When we met with our subjects, I would read the questions, Deb would take notes, and Dad's responsibility was basically to provide the comic relief. Dad's talent may span a narrow range but he is good at what he does. Then we would come home, gather around the computer, and each of us would share our thoughts about what should make the article.

LIFT OFF ~ The initial game plan was to have my series run for a few weeks within the format of Deb & Dad's feature which appears on the back page of the *Sentinel* every week. But the whole thing just kind of exploded.

More and more people wanted to participate and when we started to turn our material into my boss, Chris Carosa, he made the decision that he thought my column should run concurrently, in addition to Deb & Dad's!

So, we spent the summer of '17 trolling the town, generating material and on September 21, 2017 "Skyler Smith's Tour of Mendon" made its debut. The degree to which the scope of the project changed over time is truly mind-blowing. After attaining the status that it would be its own entity, the initial hope was that we could generate enough material for my column to last through all of 2017.

GOAL POSTS ~ The good news became that we managed to keep moving the goalposts farther and farther back. When we got into 2018, the next goal was that we could keep it going through my graduation that June.

After realizing that goal, we then hoped we could continue through calendar year 2018. Once we cruised into 2019 the consensus was that it would find its own natural conclusion. At this point the initiative was going to be chalked up in the win column no matter how it played out.

GOING OUT ON TOP ~ During my senior year in high school I was the only kid in the class who had his own weekly column in the local newspaper. There's nothing like that to establish some immediate cred in the hallowed high school hallways.

Once we realized we would be in the ballpark of 100 columns that seemed to validate the "Hiatus at a Hundred" concept. So I may ramble a bit over these final few weeks but I feel confident my audience will bear with me as I wax nostalgic over this rewarding interaction I have shared with my community.

Next week I'll be back to share bits and pieces of some of my favorite stories including The Mendon Tavern, the Black Horse Bistro, and the *Sentinel* with my boss Chris Carosa.

IT'S WEEK 97, AND I'M STILL IN HEAVEN

As I shared with you last week I'm in the process of putting my current column on hiatus. "Skyler Smith's Tour of Mendon" debuted in September of 2017, and since then I have taken you all on an extensive tour of the hamlet and its surroundings.

I have announced that I'm going on hiatus after column #100 for a well-deserved rest. My final columns of this initial run will share the highlights of my most well-received previous installments. As I would often say when Deb, Dad and I left for an interview, "The Terrific Trio rides again!" and as Deb would often say when we would start one of our adventures, "Here we go!"

CHRIS CAROSA ~ Man I was sweating bullets on this one. An interview with my boss … what could possibly go wrong? Screw this one up and the next thing I know I'm reassigned to writing obituaries. Talk about pressure. Today I'm riding high, on top of the literary world, and under Pulitzer consideration for authoring one of the most talked about breakthrough columns of the year. But fame can be fleeting; one minute I'm writing the "Skyler Smith's Tour of Mendon" column and the next minute I'm doing "Skyler Smith's Tour of the Graveyard."

MENDON TAVERN ~ One of my favorite articles I worked on was the one about Ye Mendon Tavern because I was already good friends with the proprietor Pat Freeman. She and I knew each other because she works at my high school and throughout my academic career we always had a special relationship. We always tried to help each other out and she let me address her as just "Freeman."

She had no need to get all formal with that "Mrs." stuff, she's just Freeman to me. In the summer of 2017, as Freeman and I corresponded through Dad and Deb prior to meeting for our interview, Dad and Deb joked that they couldn't tell who was more excited about the encounter, me or her.

If you had to list the things that you've done every day since 1982 what would be on your list? Sure, there would be survival skills such as sleeping, eating, and breathing, but what about things that you didn't really have to do? Well, if you were Ye Mendon Tavern, you could boast that one item on your list of things you've done every day is the fact that you have been open to the public.

Proprietor Pat Freeman takes great pride in the fact that since she began to run the Tavern, it has been open every day since December 1, 1982. As of the date of publication of this article, the Mendon Tavern will have been open 13,406 consecutive days. Now that's a work ethic I can admire!

BLACK HORSE BISTRO ~ This story stood out in my mind because it happened on what may have been the busiest day in my life. The story occurred on June 12, 2015 when Deb and Dad enjoyed a surprise wedding reception at the Black Horse Bistro which was just two doors down from us in Mendon.

Their wedding had taken place at the Ganondagan Native American Historical site in Victor. The service had been presided over mutually by Ganondagan Holy Man Peter Jemison and Dad's former student R.J. Maute. My services were quadruply requested.

Talk about being totally overworked; check out my job description for the wedding day. In chronological order I served as camera man, ring bearer, best man, and witness. If there is not a child labor law on the books in New York State that covers this type of situation, there should be.

While we give the lawmakers a week to work on this one, please look forward to visiting me next week when I will be reprising highlights from my columns on the Mendon Animal Hospital, the Cottage Hotel, and the Mendon Fitness Studio.

IT'S WEEK 98, AND EVERYTHING'S GREAT

RESET ~ After writing my weekly *Sentinel* column for the past couple of years, I feel like I've reached out and touched everyone who has wanted to be touched. So after week #100 I'm going to take a well-deserved vacation. But if you're reading this and thinking that Skyler hasn't touched me yet, and I would like to be touched, just let me know. I'll always have a few stories brewing on the back burner. So as I continue to wind things down I have some more excerpts for you this week drawing upon my most well received installments.

THE COTTAGE HOTEL ~ On the topic of most bizarre story, owner Hilary Stott had one that I couldn't quite believe, and this one is more modern-day. A couple of her customers recently informed her that they were pregnant and the baby was conceived in the Cottage's parking lot! I asked her what kind of zoning was necessary to conduct that procedure on her premises. She told me she'd get back to me.

MENDON ANIMAL HOSPITAL ~ Moving on to the Mendon Animal Hospital, Dr. Gluckman shared with me his story about the smartest cat to ever live in Mendon. This jet black feline was the only animal ever shrewd enough to establish two separate identities at the vet's. At this point we will not reveal the names in order to protect the guilty.

The lucky black cat in question had managed to establish herself as the pet in two different households in somewhat close proximity. What would be the advantage to this if you're a cat? If three square meals a day sounds good, doesn't six sound even better?

But as they say, all good things come to an end. The smartest cat in town unfortunately falls victim to a wound that, while certainly not life threatening, does warrant a trip to the vet.

On a certain afternoon a family brings in their cat, Blackie, with a wound on its side. Dr. Gluckman's diagnosis is "minor wound on abdomen. No treatment necessary." The owners and Blackie go home. A couple of hours later another family brings in a black cat named Midnight which Dr. Gluckman recognizes as the same cat that he had treated earlier that day. The gig is up. The smartest cat in Mendon had been exposed!

MENDON FITNESS STUDIO ~ A good friend of mine Amir Campbell rented our little blue building for a couple of years where he operated the Mendon Fitness Studio. As part of his promotional campaign we collaborated on a photograph mimicking the 1960's

Batman TV series which Dad got me hooked on when I was just a kid and I have been a huge Bat-fan ever since. But there is one Catwoman episode that I've never completely understood. Here's the storyline.

It's right before one of the cliffhanger endings where the villain leaves Batman and Robin in the throes of certain death. I'll quote Julie Newmar's Catwoman on this one. She describes the perilous plight of the Caped Crusaders as follows, "You've been encased in an enormous echo chamber weighing two tons. Every sound will be magnified ten million times. Even your breathing will sound like thunder. And don't bother looking for your utility belt; I've had it burned."

Catwoman continues, "I'm sure you'll recognize this as a variation of the legendary Chinese water torture. When I throw that switch, the noise will become excruciating and your eardrums will be shattered. Shortly following that, your brains will be turned to mush. Then I shall return and you can be mine forever, Batman. True I'll have to sacrifice your intellect, but oh well, with a build like yours, who cares."

At this point she eyeballs Batman from head down to waist, then back up again and finishes by saying, "After all, a girl can't always have her cake and eat it too." Dad and Deb laugh so hard at that and I'm not quite sure why. They refuse to explain it to me, but if anyone out there knows what a double entendre is, please let me know.

I'll be back next week, same bat-time, same bat-channel. Please rejoin me for memories from the Dairy Shack, Mendon Pet Supply and Markus Tattoo.

IT'S WEEK 99, AND I'M FEELING FINE

As I've shared with you over the past few weeks, I'm in the process of putting my current column on hiatus. "Skyler Smith's Tour of Mendon" debuted in September of 2017, and since then I have taken you all on an extensive tour of the hamlet.

I have announced that I'm going on hiatus after column #100 for a well-deserved rest. My final columns of this initial run will share the highlights of my most well-received previous installments.

MENDON DAIRY SHACK ~ This story ended on an ironic note, and not a sweet one for me. The day I did this interview my doctor informed me that I was lactose intolerant. I closed by saying that since I would no longer be able to carry my weight in terms of supporting the Dairy Shack, I encouraged my *Sentinel* readers to step up their support and help fill the void my lactose intolerance had created.

MENDON PET SUPPLY ~ You know how anytime you're in an animal related business you can't help but get sucked in by the posters and plaques on the walls with funny animal sayings? Keeping our focus on cats and dogs here are our three favorites from this visit.

- In ancient times cats were worshipped as gods in Egypt; apparently, they have not forgotten this.
- Two fleas are coming out of a bar when one asks the other, "Do we take a dog home, or do we walk?"
- If aliens saw us walking our dogs and picking up their poop, who would they think is really in charge?

MARKUS TATTOO ~ When I visited Markus Tattoo, I continued to push the envelope in terms of my writing prowess. It was in this installment that I included my first poetry. As Dad is a former English teacher, I was aware of the lengthy structure and rhyme scheme of a Shakespearean sonnet.

However, truth be told, I've always been attracted by poetry with a more concise structure. To that end, I wrote a 12-line 3-stanza poem which accentuates the benefit of brevity. I've had to read one of Shakespeare's plays in English class every year and let's face it, even if you love Shakespeare you have to admit, sometimes the dude rambles on forever.

Personally speaking, I feel like I could have written the entire *Romeo and Juliet* balcony scene in under a hundred words. And that *Hamlet* suicide speech … if you're just going to off yourself anyway, sometimes less is more. And of course, the irony of that whole play is while Hamlet spends all his time deciding whether "to be or not to be", somebody else does the job for him and kills him in the final scene.

Having delivered this week's Shakespearean rant, allow me to return to my theme on the benefits of brevity and share my poem with you. I was able to sum up our visit to the tattoo parlor in one concise version which consisted of just 12 lines and 24 words.

Here are my directions for how to get from my house to Markus Tattoo which is owned and operated by my friend Seth Markus. It's a quick trip as we are both in the hamlet, on the south side of Rt. 251, each about 100 feet from the light, on opposite sides.

So how do you get from the Smiths' to Seth's?

> Out the door
> Turn right
> Start walking
> Check light
>
> Cross road
> Walk straight
> Needles there
> Anticipate
>
> Deb grateful
> Pain through
> She's got
> New tattoo

When I saw their tattoos for the first time, I asked Deb if it hurt. Her response was, "In all honesty, it felt like I was getting one shot after another for 45 straight minutes." Dad's expectedly nonchalant reply was, "Mine felt like it was licked on by kittens."

You didn't miss the last episodes of *M*A*S*H*, *Seinfeld*, or *The Big Bang Theory* so you definitely don't want to miss my send-off article called "Skyler Smith's Tour of Mendon: Hiatus at a Hundred!" It will feature my single most highly rated piece ever.

Because it's not like me to leave everything just hanging out there, here's your teaser. My original title for this segment was "Skyler Smith's Tour of Medieval Breasts." This original story was so well-endowed it took me three weeks to tell. Combining all of this into one buxom bombshell will certainly be a challenge but I think I just may be the man for the job. See you next week.

HIATUS AT A HUNDRED!

This is Skyler Smith signing off for now. As I've been mentioning over the past few weeks, I've decided to make my 100th installment of "Skyler Smith's Tour of Mendon" a landmark of duality. In addition to hitting the century mark I'm heading for a hiatus.

For the last few weeks, I have been sharing some highlights from my most well-received installments and that's how I'll finish up. No whimpering here; we're going to end this thing with a bang!

There was a runaway winner as to the single article about which I received the greatest amount of feedback. The people's choice was one that I called "Skyler Smith's Tour of Medieval Breasts." Read on and you'll see why it was such a fan favorite.

SAVVY NAILS ~ When Deanna Haller, a former student of Dad's and his team-teaching partner Beth Thomas, rented our little blue building near the 4-corners to operate her salon Savvy Nails, some interesting stories about Dad's English classes at Victor began to emerge. My favorite is what happened one time when the students were watching the *Romeo & Juliet* movie.

Here's the scoop. The go-to high school movie version of *Romeo & Juliet* has traditionally been Franco Zeffirelli's 1968 classic film which starred Olivia Hussey as the 14-year old Juliet. While part of my "Medieval Breasts" theme had to do with the character of the Nurse being Juliet's nursemaid, the funniest part had to do with Juliet.

Like I sometimes do in my own writing, Zeffirelli was noted for pushing the envelope of the sexual revolution. In this film he wanted to see how much he could get away with and still maintain the PG rating which would enable his film to be shown in most high schools. The key point in the story occurs when Romeo and Juliet wake up after having spent their wedding night together.

In pushing the sexual envelope, Zeffirelli threw out a caveat for each gender. When Romeo gets up that morning he walks away from the bed to the window. You've heard the term full frontal nudity; well what you see on the screen would be the exact opposite of that. It's a bare-butt bonanza.

Juliet was played by the amply endowed Olivia Hussey and, for a split second, when she gets up to say goodbye, her bountiful breasts spill out of her robe and, let me put it this way, if the movie had been made in 3-D, some people in the front row could have been seriously injured. While the view lasts only a split second, for the 14-year-old boys in that classroom it was a second that may have lived on for hours, or days, or weeks.

Deanna told me that when Dad was wrapping up class, he would usually close by asking if anybody had any questions. And Dad shared that the end of class, on what became fondly remembered as the Day of the Bouncing Boobs, was always a little different with the kids kind of looking at each other waiting and wanting to say something about the risqué shot, but not knowing how to do it without coming off as crude or crass.

So usually nothing was said, the bell rang, and the kids went on their way. But not in Deanna's class. That crafty class clown Sean Wright finally came up with the perfect way to thread the needle to refocus attention on the scene in question and not get in trouble for it. Sean raised his hand, and with perfect timing and delivery said, "Mr. Smith, was Juliet really just 14 years old?"

I hope you like this story as much as I have enjoyed writing for all of you the last couple of years. It seems strange, and a little sad, to not be leaving you with a teaser about what to be looking for in my column next week. But as I've promised, this is a hiatus and not a retirement. Deb, Dad and I have had so much fun sharing our adventures with you that we could never give it up completely. Until we meet again, take care of one another.

SHUTTLE SHENANIGANS

POINT OF VIEW ~ This next story will detail our favorite shuttle ride ever. It is characterized by a decadent dose of delightful Deb delirium as only she can deliver. In order for this next story to flow we need to switch the point of view from Tim and Deb to just Tim. So at this point, take it away Tim.

I have to tell you that my wife is one of the most intelligent women I have ever known. She taught college math in Virginia but she has a knack for occasionally displaying some airheaded antics. And when she goes in this direction you can encounter some truly rarefied air; these stories are usually classic. I occasionally tease her and tell her that someday I am going to write *The Book of Deb* which will gather together all of these anecdotes.

When we attend outdoor summer concerts our local go-to venue is called CMAC and it's located on Canandaigua Lake. We tend to be creatures of habit and our hotel choice is the Inn on the Lake. It is just worth it to us to not have to deal with driving, traffic, parking, and bumper-to-bumper exits. There is also an outdoor bar there, right on the lake, and the ambiance of the people and the summer evenings make it a great place to go after the show.

SHUFFLE TO THE SHUTTLE ~ There is a shuttle service that transports concert goers from the major Canandaigua hotels to the venue and back. Catching a shuttle to the show is usually quick and easy. Of course, it varies from show to show but, in general, the shuttles to the show are simple and smooth because, depending on how early you want to get there, people head out at a wide range of times.

The return trip is always more difficult. The fairly obvious reason is that almost everyone wants to go home at exactly the same time, right after the end of the show. This particular story takes place on the evening of a Train concert which occurred on August 24, 2016. The concert is great and this story picks up right after the show.

SHOW'S OVER ~ When we return to the shuttle drop-off/pick-up site on this particular night, there are 40-50 people waiting for rides. After seeing multiple shows at this venue, one point that we have picked up on is that, for whatever reason, the pickup point is about 50 feet away from the drop-off point, at the other side of the parking lot. So, playing a hunch and making an educated guess, rather than waiting at the drop-off point where the 40-50 people are waiting, we walk to the other side of the parking lot. We are certain many of the others are looking at us as "the clueless couple."

ALL ABOARD ~ However, our hunch proves correct; the shuttle drives by the large group of people, pulls up right next to us, the shuttle doors automatically slide open, and we scoot in. Simultaneously the large herd of people moves as one toward the shuttle. They are met by the driver who has walked around the front of the vehicle and announces to the approaching crowd, "This shuttle is only for the 13 girls in the Kent family bachelorette party heading back to the Holiday Inn."

The driver then looks to her right and notices the two of us already seated in the shuttle. Seeing us, she quickly assesses the situation, and says, "This shuttle seats exactly 15 people, the math is perfect. You two can stay and will the 13 'Kent girls' please climb aboard."

DEB'S STORYTELLING ~ The 15 seats on the shuttle are arranged in three rows of five. One quality of Deb's that has always amazed me is her ability to engage total strangers in conversation. As the shuttle pulls out, she starts to share with the three girls in our row the story of our romance, (for those of you who haven't read "About the Authors" yet, the long-story-short of it is that we dated all through high school, then didn't see each other for 40 years, reunited, and got married at an Indian reservation). Initially Deb is only speaking to the three girls in our row. Within 20 seconds the entire entourage of 13 girls is so silent you could hear a pin drop, and hanging on Deb's every word. Chicks love this story.

Deb has told the story so many times that she now has the ability to include, or exclude, certain parts in order to make the story fit precisely into whatever length of time she has to tell it. Her timing, once again, is impeccable, and the shuttle pulls into the hotel driveway just as she has reached the part where the Indian Chief is pronouncing us man and wife, and bestowing the blessings of the Great Spirit upon us.

HOTEL ARRIVAL ~ The shuttle comes to a stop in front of the hotel, and I remember briefly closing my eyes and trying to think through a game plan for part two of our night. What do we need to drop off in our room; what do we need to pick up? A few seconds later I open my eyes and realize I am the only person in the freakin' shuttle. At this point, I am thinking that I have either just crossed over into the Twilight Zone, or the drugs have finally started to take their toll.

WHAT'S WRONG WITH THIS PICTURE? ~ I look up and I do see the shuttle driver walking back across the front of the vehicle, so I am slightly reassured. But Deb is still nowhere in sight. I get up, look out the window and see Deb, like a mother hen, leading this bevy of 13 bachelorettes into the hotel for their night of partying. Here is the part where we test our readers to see how closely you have been paying attention.

Other than that Deb is completely oblivious to the fact that I am no longer with her, who recognizes what else is wrong with this picture? ... This is not our hotel! We are staying at the Inn on the Lake, not the Holiday Inn. I shout out this fact to Deb, who turns around and begins the long walk of shame back to the shuttle. As she sheepishly rejoins me she says, "This is going to make *The Book of Deb*, isn't it?" I respond, "Yes, Dear, it certainly is."

CENTERFIELD ~ PUT ME IN COACH

About 15 miles from our home there's a place called Centerfield. A century ago it was a fairly vibrant little village with a small variety of commercial establishments. But with the advent of the automobile a lot of those little villages became defunct from a commercial perspective. There are 35 people who live in Centerfield but the businesses are all gone.

Probably in deference to history, the state still has road signs proclaiming "CENTERFIELD" about 300 yards apart on either side of the old village. For a few years, every time we would pass these signs we would half-jokingly throw out the notion that we should stop and get a picture with us, and the sign in the background. We had a couple of reasons, in addition to the quirkiness of the name.

One was that since we try to be adventurous, you could look at the picture and say, "There are Tim and Deb out in Centerfield again." The second reason was the connection to the John Fogerty baseball song "Centerfield" (Put me in Coach, I'm ready to play, today, look at me, I could be, Centerfield). We had actually traveled to Cleveland earlier in the summer to see Fogerty, who founded Creedence Clearwater Revival in the late 1960's before going solo.

So, after having jokingly made this comment to each other a dozen times, we decide to take the joke seriously; if for no other reason than not to hear each other repeat the joke every time we drive by. So the next time we pass through Centerfield we pull over to the side of the road as we approach the sign.

Here is an inside tip for anyone out there who has the idea of getting a picture in front of one of those roadside signs. Those things are a lot higher up than they look to be when you are just driving by. We get out of the car and crunch through about ten yards of knee-high weeds to make our way to the sign.

Trouble soon ensues. We have recently purchased a selfie stick, which was a good thing because the sign is so high that without the selfie stick, the angle would have been difficult to achieve. But we cannot get the selfie stick to work, and have to revert to attempting to take the selfie in the old fashion style, just holding the camera in our hands.

Obviously, this is a situation where no one else will happen to come walking by, to snap the picture for us because we are standing in a field in the middle of nowhere. At this point, we find ourselves struggling with two problems; the sign is so high it is difficult to get the correct angle, and the other problem is that the sun is in our eyes and on the few occasions that we get the angle right we are both squinting. Here a light bulb goes off over Tim's head and he says to Deb, "Let's go take the picture at the other sign." We are on an east/west road, it is late afternoon, we are looking directly back into the sun. If we go to the other sign, we can at least take the sun problem out of the equation.

Deb says, "Tim that is a great idea, let's do it!" So at this point we both start walking … in opposite directions. On Tim's way to the car he turns around to see where Deb is going and he's thinking, "She is not planning to walk 300 yards to the other sign, is she?" He watches as Deb walks to the sign post, takes one step beyond it, cranks her neck to see the sign's backside, and looks up expecting to see the other "Centerfield" sign.

Smitty says to her, "Deb, Centerfield is small, but not so small that the coming and going signs are on opposite sides of the same post." Deb says, "This is going to make the "Book of Deb" isn't it?" Tim replies, "Yes, Dear."

DAVID GRANT WRIGHT'S DOWNRIGHT GREAT READ

After a 33-year teaching career, Tim certainly has some stories to share and most of them stem from his academic assignments. But Tim was also the captain of the soccer team at the University of Rochester and he went on to become the first varsity soccer coach at Victor, NY during the beginning of his teaching career. Ironically, the greatest success to emerge from the student athletes he coached was David Grant Wright who went on to an accomplished acting career during which he has appeared in a few hundred movies, TV shows, and commercials.

When the 40th anniversary of the Victor Boys' Soccer Program occurred in the fall of 2018, the original coach and team members were invited back for the event. Inspired by this reunion, Tim and David collaborated on a commemorative article. Here's the opening of that piece.

As the piercing rain was pelting the pitch that portentous afternoon, Coach Tim Smith watched as his left winger, David Grant Wright cued up a corner kick in Canandaigua. Corner kicks were David's specialty. As the coach watched, Wright lofted a booming arching drive that managed to

*elude the hands and heads of every player on the field and gently curve to
find a home, nestled into the back corner of the far side of the net.*

*At that moment the coach was thinking about how good it felt to be
assuming a 1-0 lead over an archrival. One thing the coach was certainly
not thinking was that four decades later he and his wife Deb would be
interviewing accomplished actor David Grant Wright prior to his
induction into the Victor Hall of Fame. You never know where these kids
are going to end up!*

HILARIOUS COMMERCIAL ~ After watching some of David's
highlight reels, we had a hands-down choice for his commercial which
was the funniest. It's a Bud Light commercial titled "Stranded" and it
first aired during the 2010 Super Bowl.

It starts out with the survivors of a plane wreck spread out on the
beach looking scared and disheveled. David is playing the role of the
plane's pilot. A sexy female passenger approaches the group excitedly
shouting, "Listen up, everybody; I found the plane's radio equipment. I
think we can get off this island!"

Immediately following that, another passenger, some distance down
the beach, calls out with even more exciting news, "Listen up
everybody; I found the plane's beverage cart. It's full of Bud Light!"

Pilot David initiates a party frenzy by proclaiming, "Here we go!"
Immediately all the survivors abandon the girl with the lifesaving radio
equipment and rush toward the beverage cart. The irony which is
central to the humor is of course the implication that if there's Bud
Light to be had, who wants to get rescued?

There are other humorous nuances to be enjoyed. There's a black
dude emotionally talking to a bottle of Bud Light as if he were trying to
comfort a distraught child, passionately proclaiming, "We gonna be
okay." Next, the sexy girl who found the radio equipment is on the
verge of contacting the outside world to effect a rescue when the same
dude turns her radio dial to music so people can dance.

Adding to the carnival atmosphere, partiers are lined up to take joy
rides down the plane's emergency slide. There is also a giant beer keg
functioning as a Jacuzzi. Initially you see the Jacuzzi keg occupied by a
dude and two chicks. Then Pilot David enters the screen returning to

the Jacuzzi with Bud Lights in hand. A closer examination reveals the fact that one of the chicks in the Jacuzzi is wearing David's pilot hat. Surf's Up!

THANKSGIVING EVE WITH SANTA CLAUS

CHRISTMAS KARMA ~ Talk about your Christmas karma! We have a very frosty tale to tell here but we need to fittingly frame it up first. There is a small town by the name of Seneca Falls which is located about 45 minutes east of us. This quaint community boasts a population of only 8,500 but Seneca Falls features two very unique tourist attractions.

It is the home of the National Women's Hall of Fame and back in the day Susan B. Anthony could frequently be found there. It is also the town upon which Frank Capra based his Christmas classic *It's a Wonderful Life*. And there is a museum in town devoted solely to that film.

On the day before Thanksgiving in 2017 we made appointments with the curators for both of those museums and took a day trip to Seneca Falls to work on articles for our paper. We occasionally refer to the concept of "God things" in our writing and this Thanksgiving Eve ends up falling into that category.

Immediately upon returning home, we decide to swing by our local watering hole for some holiday libations. We pull out two bar stools, sit down, slide back in, and as Christ is our witness, we find ourselves sitting down smack dap next to Santa Claus. As writers, we feel like any time you can smoothly work God, Christ, and Santa Claus into the opening paragraphs of your Christmas piece you've accomplished something special. In literary circles this is known as the tasty but terribly tricky trilogy of holy trinity triumph. To coin a phrase.

All alliteration aside, (or maybe not), let's circle back to the bar as we are oft inclined to do. Of course, we don't know we are sitting next to Santa Claus, at least not at first. Hey! It's only November so the dapper dude isn't even in uniform yet. You don't spend a day at the *It's a*

Wonderful Life Museum, and just happen to walk into a bar, and belly up next to Santa Claus, do you? That sounds more like either the beginning of a bad joke or the climax of a great *Twilight Zone* episode.

NAUGHTY OR NICE ~ We only realize we are sittin' with Santa when he leans over and mentions that, "I've been making a list and checking it twice." We should note that this comment comes totally out of the blue. Then he discretely opens his laptop and says, "I want you two to know that my "Naughty or Nice" spreadsheet enables me to confirm that you've had a very nice year."

Based upon those lines, along with his jocular nature and rotund build, we pick up on the Santa Claus-is-sitting-right-next-to-us vibe. While acknowledging that this is a distinct honor, we do throw cautious glances at one another, mutually coming to the conclusion that Santa may need to stop by the Apple Store for a checkup on his "Naughty or Nice" software app. If you've gotten this far in the book, you probably know where we are going with this. Truth be told, there's been a few times this year when we have been very naughty.

At any rate, as sometimes happens during the holidays, one thing leads to another, and before the revelry is retired, our town's local Santa Claus has excitedly extended to us the offer to join him on his float in our hometown's upcoming Christmas parade. We are all-in on the offer. And we'll finish this one with an historical quirk from 2017. What are the odds that in the same week the Russians get officially kicked out of the Olympic Games, we are officially invited to participate in the Reindeer Games?

THE GREAT AMERICAN HOTEL

Proudly operating in our community is a venerable establishment known as the American Hotel. Having been around in one form or another since the late 1700's, it is drenched with an air of quaint old-fashioned small-town Americana. It sits at the four corners in the small village of Lima which boasts a population of 2,100.

The three-story brick building functions as follows. The top floor is occupied by the Reynolds family which has owned and operated the American Hotel for 100 years now. The second floor has seven rooms that are still available for overnight accommodations. This in and of itself is part of the anomaly. Towns as small as Lima no longer need hotels. After all, the stagecoach hasn't passed through in over 100 years. You don't go to Lima unless you know somebody there and subsequently you already have a place to stay.

The hotel stays afloat by virtue of the bar and restaurant that occupy the first floor. This area looks much the same as it did 100 years ago when the Reynolds first bought it and part of the attraction is that merely by entering the establishment one can feel an almost Twilight Zone-like vibe. It's as if the electric streetlight on the corner has morphed into an old-time gas-fueled lantern and you've somehow traveled back in time.

As is often the case with old buildings owned by old families, there is a cavalcade of haunting old stories. There were a dozen that we shared when we wrote our feature on the American Hotel and we are going to pick our favorite three for this book.

#1 ~ THE IRISH WAKE ~ This is one where we basically just liked the semantics. In sharing the story of his family's emigration from Ireland, owner Pat Reynolds used an expression we had not heard before. If there was such a thing as a Masters of Propagation Degree, the Reynolds family would have quantitatively qualified. Pat's grandfather was one of 16 children born in a 20-year span.

As Pat only half-jokingly conveyed to us, the Irish family approach during that era was that as the children, especially the boys, approached adulthood you pushed them out the door in order to make room for the next wave of kids.

So, when Pat's grandfather hit 18 years of age, they held an "Irish wake" for him. While this was not necessarily good news, it was considerably better news than a traditional wake. An Irish wake might be bizarrely compared to a bon voyage party. It was an Irish tradition that preceded a family member leaving for America, and very possibly never being seen by the family again.

#2 ~ MURAL MENAGERIE ~ In 1937 an itinerant artist named Higgins stayed at the American Hotel for a number of weeks. When the time came to check-out, Higgins did not have the money to pay the bill. At that point the artist negotiated a deal with Pat's father John whereby he would paint a series of landscapes in exchange for the money owed. Apparently feeling like something was better than nothing, John accepted the deal.

So, impoverished he couldn't afford to buy canvas, the landscape paintings that Higgins had promised turned into murals that were actually painted onto the dining room walls. There are nine of them altogether and they form an eye-level ring completely around the perimeter of the dining room. Upon completion of the murals, Higgins returned home to his wife and nine kids in Albany.

Current co-owner Rose Reynolds openly admits that she was never a major admirer of the murals, but her father John loved them. Loved them so much in fact that he hired a carpenter to build wooden frames around each one of the murals. The result is an effect we never noticed until it was pointed out to us.

If you sit in that dining room and just casually look around, the naked eye sends a message to your brain conveying the concept that these are framed pictures hanging on the wall. Once you know the truth, they never quite look the same again. Pat jokes with us that he loves the concept because he never has to straighten the picture frames.

Now this much, in and of itself, would already be classic American Hotel history but as is often the case with the hotel, the best part of the story is yet to come.

PAINT JOB ~ Over the years the dining room was occasionally repainted. Every time that process rolled around, Rose would try to talk her father into painting over the murals, but he had grown attached to the artwork and always rebuked Rose's requests.

Then in 1982 a reporter from the Rochester newspaper visited to do a story on the hotel. Included in the feature was the storyline behind the murals which we've shared with you here.

As it turned out, by that time Higgins had a grandson living in the Rochester area who was of course surprised to find out that some of his grandfather's artwork was on local display and had been for decades. Higgins' grandson subsequently visited the hotel and was able to recognize and verify the distinctive style of the family art. And there's more.

Turns out that after returning to Albany from Lima, the original Higgins went on to achieve a fairly significant level of renown in the art world. He was actually commissioned to paint the very last portrait of famous artist Grandma Moses and Higgins also served as a pallbearer at Grandma Moses' funeral, as well as serving in that same capacity at the funeral of oil tycoon J. Paul Getty.

So now added to the dilemma of the American Hotel mural saga is the fact that, Rose's artistic reviews notwithstanding, the paintings are worth something. And the good news is the hotel never has to worry about some scheming scalawag scarfing a picture off the wall and making off with it!

#3 ~ HOTEL HOSPICE ~ This next story takes place during the late 1970's. One day a couple, ballpark 30 years old, comes in, orders two drinks, then goes and sits at a table. Pat and his father John are working the bar that day. As John is making the drinks, Pat notices the wife leave the table to go look out the window. Shortly thereafter, Pat notices the husband lean over and is wondering what's going on.

Upon investigation, it is determined that the husband is dead. In a memo not often heard at the hotel, word goes back to the bar that, "We have a dead body at Table 2." Now you're probably thinking that the next direction in which this story is heading will be the traumatized reaction of the wife, right? Well, not so quick.

When made aware of her husband's passing, the wife's response is, "We were actually expecting this; do you happen to have a sheet to put over him?"

PERTAINING PREVIOUS PROTOCOL ~ This is not a situation that the Reynolds family has drilled for. In the uncertainty of the moment the police are called and John finds a sheet to cover the corpse.

Processing his options on the fly, John seizes upon the notion that the sheet comes up short as a strategy. Regardless of how quickly the ambulance arrives a covered corpse at table #2 is probably not the ambiance for which they are aspiring.

So, what does John do? He heads to table #2, clutches the body and manages to muscle it across the hallway to the hotel office where he props it up on the best chair in the house. He's hoping no new guests arrive at this time to check in. He's also thinking that in his long hotel career this particular "check out" that he's just processed clearly goes down as unparalleled by any other.

At this point we're sure our astute readers have logically landed on the last word that this is one story that we will not be able to spin into a happy ending. But hold on. They wouldn't call us the (Word)Smiths for nothin', would they? So let's think this over and see if we can't come up with an angle where we can send our guests home happy.

To review:
Couple new
Table 2
Order drinks
Dude sinks
Then dies
Sheet flies
Corpse rise
Eulogize

Guess that pretty much does it. Remember how the wife did not seem very upset about the sudden passing of her husband. In our search for the holy grail of a happy ending we'll go with this ... as the wife begins her joyful period of mourning, when the drinks arrive, she'll have two instead of one! Only at the American Hotel!

CHAPTER 12
FALLING FOR NIAGARA FALLS

THE BAD-NEWS BEAR
JOINS THE JERSEY JUMPER

Before anyone ever went over Niagara Falls in a barrel, the first daredevil to ever achieve fame at this site of one of the Seven Wonders of the World was a New Jersey gentleman named Sam Patch. In the early 19th century, he actually became the first daredevil to achieve national fame.

Sam Patch was born in Pawtucket, Rhode Island in 1807. Even as a child he tested his ability to jump into bodies of water from ever increasing heights. By his early 20's he began to advertise and attract crowds for his stunt jumping. By 1827 he had jumped off the 80-foot-high Passaic Falls in New Jersey and in 1828 he achieved his first 100-foot jump in Hoboken, NJ, leaping off the mast of a ship. His newly acquired nickname of "The Jersey Jumper" was well deserved.

Stories of Patch's jumps began to fill newspapers across the country and he became somewhat of a national hero. Then, in October of 1829, Sam would accept the greatest challenge of his jumping career. Invited to upstate New York, by a group of hotel owners, Patch's next stunt would be to jump into the Niagara River gorge by Niagara Falls. On October 24th, he ascended a platform 130 feet above the river, kissed the American flag, and saluted the huge crowds of fans which had assembled on both the Canadian and American sides. Patch then dropped 130 feet and disappeared into the water below.

There was a moment of anxious silence, with a boat circling near the entry point, but Patch did not resurface. Eventually, the crowd erupted in tumultuous applause when they spotted Patch, already standing on the shore. Just to prove it wasn't a fluke, Patch again performed the stunt 10 days later in front of an even larger crowd estimated at nearly 10,000 people.

With his fame now at an all-time high, Patch headed to Rochester, NY which was on his route back to New Jersey. Patch's challenge in Rochester was the 99-foot High Falls of the Genesee River. On November 6, 1829, Patch went out on a rock ledge in the middle of the falls in front of a crowd of 7,000 spectators.

Part of the showmanship that Patch had developed was that he sometimes threw his pet bear cub into the water before him. Clearly PETA was merely a glimmer in someone's eye at that point, and the bear was included in Patch's first Rochester performance. He threw the bear off the ledge and after his plunge, the crowd applauded as the cub swam safely to shore. Never one to let a bear cub steal his thunder, Patch successfully followed by jumping himself.

Looking to cash in even further on his success, Patch scheduled another High Falls jump, just one week later, fatefully, on Friday the 13th, in November of 1829. By constructing a 25-foot stand he increased the height of the jump to 124 feet. Over 8,000 Rochesterians assembled for the event. Mercifully the bear was not included in this performance for reasons we will cover later, but unmercifully the jump was to be Patch's last, the last patch, so to speak.

The secret to Sam Patch's jumping success was that he always kept his body rigid like a torpedo, and entered the water feet first. Halfway through this final jump it was clear that something was not right; his body contorted into an awkward position, he smashed into the water like never before, and did not resurface. There were multiple theories about what went wrong.

#1) Some witnesses thought they saw him slip as he left the platform.

#2) There was a medical theory floated that his body could have been affected by the change in temperature of the colder air. But, personally we are lining up behind theory number three.

#3) We think the bear pushed him. Related to our support of this theory is the original flyer circulated in Rochester during that week in November 1829. The flyer indicates that the order of the stunts had been reversed from the week before. Rather than the bear going first and Patch following, the flyer clearly states that Sam is scheduled to jump at 2:00 pm, with the bear to follow at 3:00.

Imagine this hypothetical conversation between Sam and the bear which probably precedes the push of Patch as the pair are perilously perched on the platform with the two o'clock hour approaching.

Bear: Now let me get this straight; you are going to jump at 2:00 pm and then climb all the way back up here to throw my ass off at 3:00?

Sam: That's the plan.

Bear: And 99 feet wasn't high enough for you? You've done gone and built a damn 25-foot high platform so I'm going to hit the water even harder.

Sam: That's show biz.

Bear: Sam, look down, I think your shoe is untied. Geronimo! … I've just jarred and jostled the Jersey Jumper into the Genesee. Justifiable gesture? You be the judge.

Two days later Sam Patch's body was found and he was buried in Rochester, at the Charlotte Cemetery.

NAVIGATING NIAGARA FALLS

FREE FALLING ~ We live about 90 minutes from Niagara Falls and over the years have made the trip dozens of times, mostly to see concerts. In navigating Niagara Falls there are multiple mentions of folks going over the falls in a barrel. A few years ago we were motivated to research the history of this topic and write about it. Our comprehensive overview ran for three weeks in our paper and we are going to share with you here just the most tantalizing tales.

First off we need to establish some parameters. In an historical analysis of all the people who have ever gone over Niagara Falls, you can basically divide them into three categories:

- Suicides.
- Victims who were swept over by accident.
- Daredevils who went over on purpose.

Our discussion here will focus solely on those individuals who fall into the third category above. Here's a quick overview for you. Beginning with Annie Edson Taylor in 1903, daredevils have made 17 attempts to go over Niagara Falls in a barrel, or some other device. Sixteen different people have made the attempt and the reason these numbers don't match is that some people tried it more than once and some people went over with partners.

WHAT ARE THE ODDS? ~ So we're sure a question going through your head right now is that if you decide to become the 17th person to give this thing a go, what are your odds of survival? Actually, they are higher than you might expect with 10 of the 16 folks in the barrel brigade having survived the plunge. If you're a numbers geek that comes out to 62.5%.

Before we get to our most stupendous stories, here are some related number nuances. Three people went over twice and there were a couple two-person pair-plunging teams. These crazy-ass people were all white except for one, two were women, and, PETA be damned, two people actually sent their pets over. In addition to the ever-popular barrel contraption, the free fall has also been attempted with a kayak, a jet ski, a big bouncing rubber ball and, believe it or not, one dude actually went over with nothing at all. We'll share his fate in the following pages.

The age of the people who went over ranges from 22 to 63 but here's a stumper for you. The oldest living creature to go over the falls in a barrel was 150 years old. All of which, we realize, leaves us with some explaining to do, so let's have at it.

FALLS' FIRST ~ As we splash back in time, this achievement goes to a retired school teacher whose name is Annie Edson Taylor. On October 24, 1901, her 63rd birthday, Annie goes over the falls in a barrel and survives. After being removed from the barrel her comment on the adventure is, "I would sooner walk up to the mouth of a cannon, knowing it was going to blow me to pieces, than make another trip over the falls."

She uses a custom-made barrel constructed of oak and iron, padded with a mattress. If you are a PETA member, please skip to the beginning of the next paragraph at this point. For those of you still with us, here's why. Two days before Annie's plunge, she puts her cat, Lucky, into the barrel and, in an apparent attempt to see if the cat is aptly named, Annie sends Lucky over the falls to test the strength of the barrel and see if the apparatus will survive the plunge.

Okay for you PETA people who are rejoining us now, we have mostly good news; 17 minutes after taking the plunge Annie and Lucky are reunited and posing for pictures. Annie is beside the barrel and Lucky is on top of it. Despite the fact that Lucky's head is bleeding, her allotment of nine lives has remained intact.

Two days later it is Annie's turn. Her barrel is lowered over the side of a rowboat and Annie climbs in. She is set adrift off of Goat Island and the upper rapids whisk her quickly toward the falls as the incredulous crowd witnesses a barrel containing a human being disappear over the brink of Niagara Falls for the very first time.

Less than 20 minutes later Annie's barrel is retrieved from the lower rapids. Upon opening the barrel, Annie emerges relatively unscathed except for a small gash on her head, ironically leaving Annie and Lucky in a position to compare their similar injuries as they pose for a second photo opportunity.

FIRST TO DIE ~ This "honor" goes to Charles Stephens, a rugged 58-year-old barber who died on July 11, 1920, after going over the falls in a heavy wooden barrel. The moral of his story is … pay attention to your predecessors and pay attention in physics class. A decade earlier, Bobby Leach had been the second daredevil to navigate the falls and survive, and Stephens ignores Leach's advice to test the barrel before going over.

Stephens designs his barrel using an anvil at the bottom for ballast, to keep the barrel upright after it has plunged. Had he followed Leach's advice and tested the barrel, he would have discovered that the anvil is so heavy that it will break through the bottom of the barrel.

Unfortunately, by not ascertaining this tragic reality prior to his plunge, Stephens dies when the anvil to which he is harnessed rips through the barrel, taking with it all of his body, except for his colorfully tattooed right arm which remains attached to a harness inside the barrel when it is recovered.

TORTOISE SHELL SOUP ~ Previously we had an owner/pet combo go over the falls separately (Annie and Lucky). Now let's move on to the first time that an owner/pet combo goes over together. Quirky set of circumstances … you are George Stathakis, a chef in Buffalo, you have a 150-year-old pet tortoise named Sonny, and you come to the conclusion that you and your tortoise need to cement the bond by going over Niagara Falls together. This may be the former teachers in us coming out, but right now we want to pose a multiple-choice question to our readers. Who do you predict will survive the plunge over the falls?

A) George and Sonny both survive.
B) George survives, Sonny dies.
C) George dies, Sonny survives
D) George and Sonny both die.

At this point please lock in your answers from the choices above and continue. On July 4, 1930, Buffalo chef George Stathakis straps himself and his pet tortoise Sonny into a 1000-pound wooden barrel which is 10-feet long and 5-feet in diameter. George unfortunately ignores the warning of advisors that the barrel is too big and too heavy.

When George and Sonny go over the falls their barrel survives relatively unscathed, but unfortunately, and probably because of the weight, it becomes the only barrel ever to end up lodged behind the falls. The barrel cannot be retrieved for 18 hours and George only has enough oxygen for 8 hours. Although he survives the initial fall, George dies of suffocation.

In a significant side note, apparently you don't live to be a 150-year-old tortoise without having a lot of free time to practice holding your breath. Sonny has obviously gotten very good at this because he survives the ordeal. All of which makes the correct answer to the above multiple-choice question letter "C."

THE ROCKETMAN ~ The 15th attempt to survive a trip over the falls takes on an approach different from anything previously attempted. On October 2, 1995 a 39-year-old California stunt school graduate, (Do we really need schools for this?) Robert Overacker, devises a plan to sneak a jet ski into the Niagara River, navigate it over the falls, and use a rocket-propelled parachute strapped to his back to float gently to the water below. The approach cleverly clicks as unique because Overacker is the first person to plan on taking a slow ride down from the top of the falls. It looks good on paper, and if everything goes as planned it will be the safest descent ever.

Here's how this one plays out. If this were a Road Runner cartoon, Overacker would be cast as Wile E. Coyote and the rocket-propelled parachute, which would have been made by ACME, of course fails to open. Picture the Coyote gradually getting smaller in size as he plummets to a rough landing at the bottom of the canyon. If you had an overhead view of this thing, that's what Overacker would have looked like as he plummeted to his death in the rapids below.

Of course, in the Warner Bros. cartoons, the Coyote always returns unscathed in the next scene. Unfortunately, for Overacker, this is not a cartoon and, playing upon the animation analogy theme, when The Maid of the Mist retrieves his body he is as dead as Bambi's mother.

WORST DRINKING GAME EVER ~ The final attempt to make our list is also a very unique one and it is the third in a row without a barrel. The attempts go from a kayak, to a jet ski, to nothing. On October 22, 2003, Kirk Jones becomes the first person to survive the drop without any aid whatsoever. As an afternoon party begins, Jones and his friends have set up shop on Table Rock along the bank of the river, about 25 feet above the falls. After some hard drinking, what had begun as a crazy joke somehow morphs into a good idea. Jones decides he is going to swim over the falls and have his friends videotape the stunt.

Okay here is our last interactive guessing game of this segment. At this stage of the story, pick which task is most likely to go wrong ... the swim over the falls or the video recording of the event. Maybe you predicted where we are going with this but, irony of ironies, Jones survives the plunge over the falls, but his friends are too drunk to get the camera working.

Upon reuniting with his friends, imagine the excruciating look on Jones' face when his alleged cameraman informs him, "Hey, Kirk, uh, I hate to say this, but we need a do-over." Unfortunately, the do-over is not going to be an option. Jones, who survives with only minor rib injuries, is arrested, fined $3000 and banned for life from ever reentering Canada.

When we originally wrote this piece in 2017 our stats stood as follows. At that point, of the 16 daredevils who had intentionally gone over Niagara Falls, surprisingly 11 had survived. Don't know if it's karma or chemistry, but when we get involved in a topic, strange things seem to happen. After a 14-year gap, the aforementioned Kirk Jones manages to sneak back into Canada and try it again on April 19, 2017.

Too bad for him that Canadian customs doesn't do a better job of keeping him out of the country because the inflatable ball Jones uses in his final attempt is recovered at the base of the falls that day and his body washes up two months later. Ironically Jones fared better when he went over the falls without a device.

So, in summary, here are the final statistics of the Niagara Falls daredevils scorecard from 1903 to the present. During that time period 16 people have combined to make 18 attempts to go over the falls with 10 survivors. If our tantalizing tales and the surprising survival rate of 62.5% encourage you to make your own attempt to join the barrel brigade, please keep us posted and we promise to include your addendum in the second printing of our book.

CHAPTER 13
SPORTS SPECTACULARS

IT'S A NUMBERS GAME

Here is a story that has never been brought to the public light as far as we know. You're going to hear it from us first, kids. As you read on, the reasons why will become obvious. In a way it falls under the concept of "sports bloopers" but not in the conventional sense.

This story dates back to 1993 and emanates from a WPIX broadcast of a New York Yankees baseball game. Two mainstays on the announcing crew from back in the day were Bobby Murcer and Phil Rizzuto.

Nicknamed the "Scooter," Rizzuto's catch phrase was "Holy Cow," and if somebody did something he didn't agree with, the offender would immediately be labeled a "huckleberry"; a bit archaic by modern-day standards, but he was old-school conservative and those expressions fit him. He had played for the Yankees from 1941-1956 and was a broadcaster from 1957-1995.

During the latter part of his career he became a bit absent-minded which was perhaps not surprising as he didn't retire till he was almost 80. It also became a pattern for him to leave the broadcast booth for somewhat extended periods of time, apparently just to visit folks, and eventually meander back to contribute some color commentary.

It wasn't that big of a deal, because the rest of the announcing team was certainly capable of carrying the weight on their own. By this stage of the game, Rizzuto had become such a Yankee icon that the organization felt that his foibles were a small price to pay for his continued involvement with the team.

At this point, let us set the stage for this one game in July of 1993. It is Old-Timer's Day at Yankee Stadium so all the legendary greats are on hand. Bobby Murcer and Phil Rizzuto happen to be the only two regular announcers broadcasting this particular game.

During the game, Yankee pitching legend Whitey Ford visits the broadcast booth for a period of time and the conversation turns to numerology. It is a logical progression because the New York Yankees have more retired numbers than any team in professional sports.

Murcer's personal Yankee numerology is unique in that when he first came to the majors in 1965, he was heralded as the next Mickey Mantle (they both hailed from Oklahoma) and rewarded as such with the uniform number 1. That number had become available upon the retirement of Bobby Richardson the year before.

Murcer was subsequently traded from the Yankees in 1975 and didn't return until 1979. During that interim, Manager Billy Martin had taken the number 1. So, when Murcer returned he wore number 2.

All of this number talk evolved into a conversation amongst the three players discussing the concept of whether, if they had the choice, they would change the number they wore. Ford, Murcer and Rizzuto all went on record as saying they would stick with their original numbers and the whole discussion provided Rizzuto with an excuse to, yet again, leave the booth. At the end of the inning when Whitey Ford said he was going to the clubhouse to see Mickey Mantle, Rizzuto said he would go with him because he wanted to ask Mantle if he would have kept his number 7 if he had the chance to do it all over again.

So, Rizzuto is gone for a couple of innings and upon his return it is business as usual with the broadcast until Murcer remembers that Rizzuto had planned to ask Mantle about his uniform number. When Murcer prompts Rizzuto on this topic it leads to the airing of one of the greatest practical jokes of all time.

Rizzuto enthusiastically informs the entire Yankee nation that, "Holy cow, you are not going to believe what Mickey said. He said if he had it all to do over again, he would love 69. Do you believe it! Number 69! That huckleberry said he wanted 69!" Rizzuto got the number out there five times before someone was able to put the kibosh on his numerical rant.

Just to confirm, Rizzuto certainly had no idea that he had been set up by Mantle who was known for his risqué behavior and pranks. At this point of the storyline, one can't help but ponder how two pieces played out in the aftermath.

- What was Rizzuto's reaction upon hearing the explanation for why his number 69 spiel was cut short?
- What was Mantle's reaction upon hearing that his set up of Rizzuto had been broadcast live to 100,000 people?

We're sure that the next time Rizzuto and Mantle came together, Mickey would have been greeted with a stern, "Why you huckleberry!"

For obvious reasons this will always remain one of those sports blooper highlights that will be forever buried in the vaults of time. Upon reflection, it could be considered offensive on two different levels. In addition to the obvious sexual reference, there's also the element of taking advantage of the elderly. This would be one of the greatest and last lines the merry prankster Mickey Mantle would add to his resumé. When he died just a few years later in 1995, he left us with the classic quote, "If I'd known I was going to live this long, I would have taken better care of myself."

HOCKEY HIGHLIGHTS

If you're a hockey fan, or even if you're not, we hope you'll enjoy this hat trick of humor. After a deep delve into the history of hockey here is our take on the three funniest stories in the annals of the sport.

FAVORITE HOCKEY QUOTE EVER ~ Phil Esposito was known as one of the most arrogant and funny players ever. He broke in with the Chicago Black Hawks, midway through the 1964 season and subsequently spent the best years of his career with the Boston Bruins.

He tells this story about his first NHL game which should have been the first time he took the ice, but turned out not to be. Here's why … Esposito is riding the bench for almost the entire game in which the Black Hawks are losing 7-2 against Montreal. With three minutes remaining, Coach Billy Ray looks down the bench and yells, "Esposito, get out there!" The ever arrogant and sarcastic Esposito shouts back,

"Okay, Coach, do you want me to win it or just tie it up?" Unamused, Coach Ray yells, "Sit back down."

BEST RUSSIAN SEX SCANDAL ~ The stars of this scandalous story are Sergei Fedorov and Anna Kournikova. Here are brief bios of the co-starring cast characters. Fedorov became one of the first Russian hockey players to defect, walking away from Team Russia during the 1990 Good Will games in Portland, Oregon. After joining the Detroit Red Wings, he led the team to three Stanley Cup championships over the next 12 years.

Kournikova was a beautiful Russian tennis player who, after her stellar performance in the 1996 US Open, vaulted her world ranking from #144 to #69. Keeping in mind the numerology from our previous segment, you gotta love the math of where that one lands!

During the same year, Fedorov and Kournikova meet at the 1996 Olympic Games in Atlanta. Subsequently, romantic rumors resonate. But with Kournikova, only 16 years old, and Fedorov 28, the couple issues more denials than serves or slap shots. Years later they are eventually married, and divorced, but the initial stages of their courtship are a tabloid topic of the era.

Our vote for the funniest media moment on the topic occurs on *The Late Late Show with Craig Kilborn*. On his June 7, 1999 show, Kilborn notes that it is Kournikova's 18th birthday. After a pregnant pause, Kilborn finishes his monologue with the punch line, "Or as hockey player Sergei Fedorov knows it, 'The day I can legally start telling everyone that I am sleeping with Anna Kournikova.'"

While in Hockey's Hall of Fame, Fedorov may well also be in Russia's Hall of Shame. Will there ever be anyone else in Russian history who manages to both defect the National Hockey Team and defile the National tennis star? Ironically, Tim has just decided to start his own Hall of Fame and has declared Fedorov to be the first inductee.

MOST WELL ADJUSTED PRIORITIES ~ Appearing on *The Dick Cavett Show* in the 1970's, Gordie Howe, aka Mr. Hockey, was asked by Cavett why hockey players always wear protective cups, but at that time few wore helmets. Howe's humorously blunt response was,

"You can always get someone else to do your thinking for you." Tim has just made Gordie Howe his second inductee.

THE SIMPSONS ~ ALL ABOARD FOR ALBUQUERQUE

MINOR LEAGUE BASEBALL ~ Unless you follow baseball very closely this is a story you probably haven't heard before and it has three characteristics which, if they all can be said about a given story, tend to create a winner. Our three winning characteristics are that if a story can be bizarre, funny and also true, chances are you've got a good one on your hands.

Especially when you get to the minor leagues in various sports, there are some unusual team nicknames floating around out there. Our vote for best story in that category is the Los Angeles Dodgers' Triple A franchise which plays in Albuquerque, New Mexico. In 2003 this franchise migrated south from Canada where they were known as the Calgary Cannons.

A media panel had selected that nickname because the alliteration sounded nice and when it was chosen no other professional or college teams in North America were called the Cannons. But Albuquerque had no particular affinity for "Cannons" and the alliterative appeal was lost, so it was decided that there would be a contest for the city to pick a new nickname for its baseball team. This is where the story gets a bit strange.

THE SIMPSONS ~ A few years prior to this contest, on March 4, 2001, the Fox Network had aired an episode of *The Simpsons* called "Hungry, Hungry Homer," in which Homer Simpson spearheads a movement to keep his hometown baseball team, the Springfield Isotopes, from moving to New Mexico and becoming the Albuquerque Isotopes.

The show is set in the fictional town of Springfield and according to the storyline, their minor league baseball team is the Springfield Isotopes. If you watch *The Simpsons* you'll get the gag of that unusual nickname. In the show, Springfield is home to a nuclear power plant at which Homer works, hence the appropriateness of the "Isotopes" nickname.

ALBUQUERQUE ~ As it turns out, Albuquerque apparently is home to a preponderance of Simpsons fans. The contest to select a new nickname was conducted by the *Albuquerque Tribune* and its online readers cast a remarkable 67% of their votes for the "Isotopes," mimicking the storyline of the *Simpsons* episode. So ironically, while the Albuquerque Isotopes never came to fruition in the cartoon world, the real world was blessed with the first sports team to ever base its nickname on the plot line of an animated TV series.

After the nickname was announced in 2002, the Isotopes sold more merchandise in just three months than Albuquerque's previous baseball team had ever sold in an entire year, and in 2003 they sold more merchandise than any team in minor league baseball. The nickname has stuck, and the Albuquerque Isotopes are still playing in the Pacific Coast League.

MUHAMMAD ALI ~ THE GREATEST

After visiting the Boxing Hall of Fame we were justifiably inspired to write about Muhammad Ali, who proudly proclaimed himself to be "the Greatest." He then went out and proved that to be true. The most compelling aspect of the Ali story was the impact he had on both sports and society. Toss in the fact that he was also one of the funniest human beings ever, and he earns himself a chapter in our book.

Christened with the name Cassius Clay, he first thrusts himself into the boxing spotlight by winning the gold medal in the heavyweight division at the 1960 Olympics in Rome. After beginning his professional career with a four-year undefeated streak, Clay would first fight for the heavyweight title as a 7 to 1 underdog in a 1964 boxing match with the thuggish Sonny Liston.

Before the fight, Clay, who becomes known for the incessant taunting of his opponents, dubs Liston a "big ugly bear," says he "even smells like a bear," and summarizes things by saying, "After I beat him I'm going to donate him to the zoo." And in a bearish beat down, Clay does defeat Liston, ascending to the throne of heavyweight champion.

After winning the heavyweight championship for the first time, and changing his name to Muhammad Ali, he would go on to lose the title and win it back three more times. There's one element to this storyline that we feel needs to be shared, particularly with our younger readers. A few generations ago the sport of boxing was much more ingrained in the fabric of American society. Here's one condensed way of looking at it. During the Ali era most people on the street could tell you the name of the world heavyweight boxing champion and during the current era, almost no one can. It was a time when if the Pope was walking down the street with Muhammad Ali, people would look at the pair and say, "Who's that with Ali?"

Muhammad Ali brought an energy and charisma to the sport which was never equaled before or after his career. Even his individual fights sometimes took on personalities of their own. There was the "Thrilla in Manila" with Joe Frazier and "The Rumble in the Jungle" with George Foreman where Ali coined the phrase "rope-a-dope" to describe the strategy he employed to defeat the bigger, stronger Foreman.

He often waxed poetic as in the following lines he wrote describing his pugilistic prowess:

> I've wrestled with alligators,
> I've tussled with a whale.
> I done handcuffed lightning
> And thrown thunder in jail.
> You know I'm bad.
> Just last week, I murdered a rock,
> Injured a stone, Hospitalized a brick.
> I'm so mean, I make medicine sick.

His whimsical war of words with sports announcer Howard Cosell can be revisited in all its YouTube glory. His epic quotes were epitomized by his analysis of his own boxing style and success ... "Float like a Butterfly, Sting like a Bee" and "I am the Greatest!" He certainly was.

We thought we would close this segment by sharing with you our Fab Five Faves of other Ali quotes, ranging from inspirational to hilarious.

- "If you even dream of beating me, you better wake up and apologize."
- "It isn't the mountain ahead to climb that wears you out; it's the pebble in your shoe."
- "If they can make penicillin out of moldy bread, they can sure make something out of you."
- "I'm so fast that last night I turned off the light switch in my hotel room and was in bed before the room was dark."
- "Live everyday as if it were your last because someday you are going to be right."

BRAWLIN' AT THE BRONX ZOO

Whether you loved them or hated them, the late 1970's New York Yankees boasted entertainment ratings that were off the charts. The team ended what, to that point, had been the longest World Series drought in franchise history. The Yanks went to the Fall Classic three years in a row from 1976-1978, taking the series two of those three years.

But amidst the sweet smell of success, the era was also characterized by tension and turmoil. The combination of a bombastic owner, a volatile manager, and a team roster filled with controversial characters made histrionic headlines on and off the field. Cy Young Award-winning pitcher Sparky Lyle told the story in his bestselling book whose title *The Bronx Zoo,* came to deftly define the Yankees of this era.

BRONX ZOO ~ Many memorable quotes emerged from the drama. The one that probably summed it up best came from third baseman Graig Nettles who said, "Some kids dream of joining the circus, others dream of becoming major league baseball players. As a member of the New York Yankees, I've gotten to do both."

Tyrannical owner George Steinbrenner hired and fired adversarial manager Billy Martin on five different occasions by the time it was all said and done. Yankee captain and catcher Thurman Munson was a stoic hard-ass who immediately clashed with the flamboyant Reggie Jackson when he joined the team as a free agent in 1977 declaring himself, "The straw that stirs the drink," and correctly making the arrogant prediction that, "If I play in New York they'll name a candy bar after me."

Jackson did seem to be the catalyst that put the Yankees over the top. After being swept in the World Series by the Cincinnati Reds in 1976, the Yankees won the Fall Classic the next two years in a row, defeating Tommy Lasorda's Los Angeles Dodgers both times. Of the Yankees' cast of characters perhaps the most humorous, quirky and cantankerous relationship was that between center fielder Mickey Rivers and right fielder Reggie Jackson.

FUNNY QUOTES ~ The humor of Mickey Rivers came from the fact that he somehow managed to combine Yogi Berra's skewed logic with the African American experience. Using math that totally conjured up Yogi he once said, "Pitching is 80% of the game and the other half is hitting and fielding."

While summarizing how he fit into the owner/manager/player chemistry he said, "Me and George and Billy are two of a kind." Born in Miami, he had a southern boy mentality and after one cold game in Chicago his take on the weather was that, "It was so cold today that I saw a dog chasing a cat, and the dog was walking."

Rivers was perhaps the only Yankee who had the ability to get under the skin of Reginald Martinez Jackson. Prodding Reggie about his name Rivers once said, "No wonder you're all mixed up. You got a white man's first name, a Spanish man's middle name, and a black man's last name."

Probably in a bad mood, because he was mired in a rare slump, Jackson once put Rivers down, in front of reporters, by saying that he should learn how to read and write. Rivers' response to the same audience was, "Jackson better stop readin' and writin' and start hittin.'" Touché.

And our favorite ... On hearing that Reggie Jackson was reported to have an IQ of 165, Mickey Rivers contrarily replied, "Out of what – a thousand?"

COMPLICATIONS ~ It was a great little run while it lasted. In 1977 when the Yankees won their first World Series in fifteen years, the aforementioned Sparky Lyle also won the Cy Young Award as baseball's best pitcher. As if that wasn't enough, during the off season the Yankees also signed the second best relief pitcher in baseball, Goose Gossage, assuring more controversy.

Gossage was younger, stronger, and emerged as the Yankees go-to closer in 1978 leaving Lyle to spend the year complaining, while demanding more money or a trade, but receiving neither. With the extra time on his hands Lyle spent the season writing his tell-all book, *The Bronx Zoo*. Handing off the mic to Graig Nettles to wrap up this part of the story, Nettles summarized the pitching situation by saying that, "I feel bad for Sparky Lyle. He went from Cy Young to Sayonara."

BEST YANKEE STORY EVER ~ We are going to close out this segment by sharing our favorite story starring one of the Bronx Zoo characters. This story is actually set in the mid-50's and it features a young Billy Martin. The time may have been earlier, but the firecracker personality that characterized the man was unwavering, as you'll see.

The Yankees of this era were known for their hard-play, both on and off the field, and three men who were known to be at the top of that era's party list were Mickey Mantle, Whitey Ford, and Billy Martin.

This story takes place on one of the team's rare and cherished off-days during the long, grueling season. On this day the trio has made plans to go hunting on a large wooded property owned by one of Mantle's friends in the Poconos. After a two-hour drive, Mantle turns his car into the driveway of his friend's ranch, parks by a cow pasture and tells Ford and Martin to sit tight while he goes in to touch base with the owner.

Once inside, the owner reviews with Mantle the logistics of his property and where the men should go to hunt. Mantle has hunted the property before so there is nothing news-breaking about what the owner shares with him. But as Mantle turns to go, the owner does have one last rather unusual request. He says, "When you go back to your car you'll see one old horse in the cow pasture. I've had her for 25 years, she's crippled by arthritis, I need to put her down and I can't bring myself to do it. Would you take care of that for me? I'd appreciate it."

MISCHIEF IS AFOOT ‑ Taken aback a bit, but wanting to do what he can for his friend, Mantle agrees to fulfill the request. On his way back to the car, a practical joke occurs to Mantle.

Upon returning to Billy Martin and Whitey Ford, Mantle unleashes a profanity-ridden tirade of intentional fabrications, the gist of which is that his friend has changed his mind and after taking hours to drive to the Poconos, his friend has told him that they will not be allowed to hunt.

"You know what I'm going to do?" Mantle queries. "I'm going to shoot that damn bastard's horse." At that point Mantle follows through on his friend's request, firing one accurate shot to put the crippled horse down.

Immediately thereafter, Mantle hears two more shots ring out and then Billy Martin saying, "Let's get the hell out of here, I just shot two of his cows."

IS THAT AN NFL FOOTBALL PLAYER IN OUR HOUSE?

HOME SWEET HOME ‑ We live near the four corners of Mendon, a small town about 15 miles south of Rochester, New York. We used to operate a walk-in retail memorabilia store and the building still has a commercial look to it. It's set very close to the road, and is mostly glass in front, through which a lot of our personal collection is visible from the sidewalk. So, it is not at all unusual for curious passersby to walk up, press their noses to the glass, and try to figure out what in the world is going on inside.

We even have had people open the door, walk in, and ask if we are open. This has led to us providing many impromptu tours and we have made some great friends from total strangers. Here is our most classic story of somebody approaching our house out of the blue.

SURPRISE VISITOR ~ One summer day we notice a huge man lumbering across the street toward our house, press his nose to the glass, and look in. As we get up to say hi, he opens the door and asks, "What is this place?"

We offer a brief explanation and ask him if he would like a tour, which is something we often find ourselves doing. As we are moving from one exhibit to another, he notices a University of Virginia pennant and says, "I played football for Virginia." Next, he notices a picture we have of Michael Jordan in his Birmingham minor league baseball uniform and says, "I broke into professional football playing for Birmingham's team in the USFL." (The USFL was an upstart football league that competed with the NFL during the 1980's.) At this point we are hesitantly wondering if we are being played and you won't believe what happens next.

He sees a Jim Kelly-autographed Buffalo Bills football and says, "Yeah, I played with Jim on the Bills and he is still one of my best friends." So, at this point we are thinking "no freakin' way." But believe it or not, it is all true. Our unknown visitor is East Rochester native, Joe Bock, who has the unique distinction of being the only player to be Jim Kelly's teammate on both the Buffalo Bills and the USFL Houston Gamblers where Kelly started his career.

That was several years ago and in the interim we have spent many hours sharing tales and toddies with the big fellow. Joe is truly one of the zaniest characters we have ever met and when the drinks start to flow so do the stories. In terms of potential writing storylines, it was like God had blessed us. We started to collaborate with him on an article for our local paper and by the time we were done we had a 7-week series.

We have written so much about Joe that as we analyzed it in the context of this book, because every single story is so freakin' funny, it became difficult to decide which ones would make the cut for this project. Then the criteria hit us. Two of Joe's stories involved his connections with Hall of Fame athletes that sports fans would have heard of. And both of these stories are ones that, unless you know Joe, you've never heard before.

We thought that provided us with the unique opportunity to share with the world a couple behind-the-scenes sports stories and share for all posterity a few tales that would never had been told had we not written this book. No matter how much of a hardcore sports fan you are we are about to bless you with some tantalizingly untold tales.

At this point let us introduce the stars of the show. Two fellow athletes with whom Joe Bock spent significant quality time would be the Buffalo Bills' NFL Hall of Fame quarterback Jim Kelly and the Houston Rockets' NBA Hall of Fame center Ralph Sampson. And both the Kelly story and the Sampson story are so infused by Joe Bock's crazy-ass over-the-top personality that you could understand why each Hall of Famer might be a tad reluctant to have these tales go public. But here we are sitting on material like this with the knowledge that if we don't share it, we will be taking it to the grave. So what the hell, let's not save it for a death bed confession; how 'bout we smash the wine goblets against the back of the brick fireplace wall, make another drink, and let the games begin!

It was truly a coin toss to decide which Hall of Fame tell-all to begin with so we defaulted to the concept of chronological order. Joe Bock went to college at the University of Virginia where he became good friends with Ralph Sampson, and then later went on to play professional football with Jim Kelly. So, let's start out with some college fun at UVA.

VIRGINIA'S RALPH SAMPSON ERA ~ The most famous athlete at the University of Virginia when Joe was there was basketball player, Ralph Sampson. Sampson was a 7'4" center who went on to play most of his pro career in the NBA with the Houston Rockets where he paired up with Hakeem Olajuwon to form the "twin towers." He was always known to be a quiet introverted man and that was even more true when he was a young college kid. But Ralph Sampson came to share a special friendship with Joe Bock.

There was an overlap between the football and basketball teams in that they shared "training table," which meant they had meals together, and they also shared workout facilities. Joe was two years older than Ralph and intrigued by the highly touted young freshman phenom basketball player when he arrived at Virginia.

CRACKING THE SHELL ~ Despite Ralph's reluctance to engage with the other athletes, especially the non-basketball players, Joe with humor and self-confidence comes right out and says, "Ralph, you know what, I'm gonna crack your shell." Initially he doesn't get much of a response, but if nothing else, Joe is persistent.

At this point Joe decides he needs a strategy, and he comes up with a viable one. While a foot shorter than Ralph, Joe at 6' 4" was a standout high school basketball player who could handle himself on the hardwood. So initiating his newly developed strategy, Joe makes a point of sitting by Ralph at every meal he can and challenging him to a game of one-on-one basketball. Ralph always declines, but Joe's humor and persistence gradually chisel a crack in the Sampson shell.

Once Joe feels that he has sufficiently softened Sampson, he decides it is time to initiate the killer cornerstone phase of his strategy. At lunch one day, Joe imparts the following line of reasoning upon Ralph.

THE ULTIMATUM ~ Joe says, "Okay Ralph, you know I've been consistently making this request for a one-on-one faceoff between the coolest guy on the football team and the quietest guy on the basketball team. And as much as you hate to admit it, I'm beginning to grow on you. We're going to be here together for at least the next two years, three if I don't graduate on time which is a distinct possibility, and there are two ways this thing can play out. You could agree to play me today, or you could choose to have me endearingly engage you on this challenge several hundred more times."

Ralph smiles and says, with typical brevity, "Meet me at the gym at 3:00." So, after two months of begging, it's finally "Game On." As a 6' 4" center at East Rochester, Joe had a standout high school basketball career. But of course, the reality of this one-on-one matchup would seem to be a foregone conclusion. Just to reset, we've got a one-on-one basketball challenge between a 7' 4" future Hall of Fame basketball player and a 6' 4" football player whose resumé does acknowledge that he played high school hoops for ER. Here is Joe's account of the one-on-one game.

GAME ON - As the contest begins, Joe is correctly thinking that his only slim chance is to get the ball first, so he asks for that concession. Perhaps overconfident, Sampson yields the first possession to Joe.

Never one to enter an encounter without a strategy, Joe has one in place. He dribbles around the court in a semi-circle slyly calculating the distance at which Sampson is willing to extend his coverage to guard Joe. Apparently underestimating Sampson's resolve, Joe unfortunately realizes that he's going to have to retreat about 30 feet away from the basket before Sampson will back off and allow him to take an uncontested shot.

At this point, embracing the solace of the fact that Sampson has agreed to play him at all, Joe lines up a set shot and hits if from 30 feet. Contrary to all the Vegas odds, Joe has an early lead. In retrospect Joe now admits that taunting Sampson at this point with his repeated refrain of, "I'm no Delilah, I'm no Delilah," may have been ill-advised. Sampson responds by scoring 11 points in a row thus winning the game 11 to 1, but at least at one point Joe felt he had him on the ropes.

MISSION ACCOMPLISHED - And of course if you zoom out your lens of perspective on the relationship between Ralph Sampson and Joe Bock there is an irony that has been brought into focus by this one-on-one basketball game. Joe lost the game but he won the war. And in this case by "war" we are referring to Joe's greater goal which was directly stated to Ralph at the beginning of this story. Joe told Ralph "I'm gonna crack your shell," and the mere fact that the Joe versus Ralph game occurred served as proof that Joe had achieved his objective and went on to become one of Ralph's best friends at Virginia.

Joe said that a lot of people on the Virginia campus considered Sampson to be arrogant and aloof because he was quiet, kept to himself, and did not reach out to engage with the rest of the college community. Joe came to realize that while those descriptions of Sampson's behavior were accurate, the personality traits to which they were attributed were not. Sampson was not arrogant; he was a shy, quiet, introspective man who tended to stay in his shell. It was a shell he opened to very few and Joe became one of those few.

OPPOSITES ATTRACT ~ An irony about the Bock/Sampson friendship is that, other than the commonality that they were both star athletes at the University of Virginia, they were exact opposites in almost every way. While Sampson had a reserved demeanor, Joe was socially boisterous and over-the-top. Sampson was studious; Joe was a partier. Sampson was a black kid from Dixie; Joe was a white kid from New York.

Despite the fact that they were polar opposites in some ways, their mutually symbiotic friendship evolved to the point where there were multiple examples of how one came to the other's rescue. There were several occasions when Joe had partied so deeply into the night that Ralph would come across him on his way to his first class and give Joe a ride home. The best story of Joe returning the favor was when he came through for Ralph at the campus-wide graduation party which Sampson hosted.

BEST STORY OF THEM ALL ~ Of all of Joe's Virginia stories, this is our favorite. During Ralph Sampson's college career, one of Virginia's greatest star football players ever, Stuart Anderson, is drafted in 1982 by the Kansas City Chiefs, and the University puts prominent senior Ralph Sampson in charge of a campus-wide celebratory gala.

The itinerary of the party is to start with an on-campus pig roast and finish with a beer blast at University Hall, the sports arena where the Virginia Cavalier basketball team plays. For many of you in our audience who are too young to remember, the official drinking age back in the day was 18, so basically if you were old enough to be in college, you were old enough to drink especially by the **end** of your freshmen year.

BEER BATTLE ~ Joe Bock is two years older than Ralph Sampson so at this point he's playing pro football, but since this party is in May it is during Joe's off season. During that time Joe is working for Miller Beer and as you might suspect, he manages to become an integral part of the Virginia festivities.

When the party is originally scheduled, Budweiser is the first beer distributor to get wind of it and subsequently donates 30 kegs of beer as a promotional ploy. Joe's boss at Miller is disappointed that his company has been beaten to the punch for this opportunity and complains to Joe,

"You were a big star there. How does the University not go through you first?"

Joe's response is, "Don't worry. This is a blessing in disguise. In the end we're going to come out ahead on all fronts." As usual Joe is a man with a plan. And what is that plan you ask? Read on.

JOE TO THE RESCUE ~ Joe has not been removed from the University of Virginia college experience long enough to have lost touch with the pulse of the Cavalier Community. He correctly assesses the situation and comes to the conclusion that 30 kegs is not going to be nearly enough to fulfill the needs of what is scheduled to be an all-day event. Joe's plan, as he shares with his boss, is that the Miller team will lurk in the background awaiting the inevitable and preparing to pounce.

When the Bud runs out, just as Joe predicts it will, right when the party is peaking, the folks at Miller will come riding in from the sunset to save the day. And the other piece in place to perfect the plan is that, as we mentioned before, the University has put Joe's good friend Ralph Sampson in charge of the purse strings.

Around 7 pm Joe ambles into the festivities like a recent grad and sports star who's just returned to acknowledge the accomplishments of his former teammate Stuart Anderson. When it comes to beer and partying there are few people on the planet that operate on the level of Joe Bock. Just like he drew it up on the chalkboard, it's not long before he notices 7' 4" Ralph Sampson running up to him with a look of desperation on his face and saying, "We're out of beer, but we've got plenty of money, can you help?"

Joe says, "I'll take care of it with my boss. The going rate is $28.00 a keg and we'll get back here as fast as we can." At this point Joe gets into his boss's pickup truck and the pair head for the local Miller brewery. Less than half an hour later they're back to the campus and receiving a welcome worthy of conquering heroes. Picture the scene when the Santa float pulls into the Macy's parade, multiply that by ten, and you get the sense of the adulation the Miller truck receives from the Virginia kids.

VIRGINIA PARTIES ON ~ The rest of the night is a series of triumphant returns by Joe and his boss with Ralph Sampson shoving more money in their pockets upon every return. And of course, this piece is one of the great ironies of Joe's master plan. Miller is getting paid for all of the beer they're delivering while Bud gave away their 30 kegs for free.

They could get six kegs in the truck at one time and they end up bringing 28 altogether, so it involves 5 separate delivery trips and Joe conveys what you're probably anticipating on your own. The campus craziness increases with every return. On the final trips back, Joe and his boss are driving the truck right inside the arena, across the basketball court, with a sea of worshipping bodies slowly parting before them.

Also, adding to the excitement is an idea that occurs to Joe and his boss on their third beer run. While loading the truck with the six kegs per trip, they fill up the rest of the truck bed with cans of Miller and when they get to the campus, Joe climbs into the bed and immediately ascends to the status of biggest man on campus, Ralph Sampson's 7' 4" frame notwithstanding.

Picture this scene … We have a pickup truck, carrying a precious cargo of beer kegs, slowly crossing a college basketball court full of kids, who all part before the oncoming vehicle like the Red Sea parted before Moses. And all the while, Joe Bock is in the back of the truck gently tossing free cans of beer into the frenzied crowd. Joe wanted us to assure university's authorities that not one can of beer ever hit the Cavaliers' court before being snatched up by someone. As it turns out Ralph Sampson runs out of cash before he can pay for the last keg, but it is no big deal.

FINAL CAVEAT ~ And there is one final caveat to this story which doesn't happen until two years later. After this 1982 party, Ralph Sampson goes on to play pro basketball for the Houston Rockets and in 1984, as fate would have it, Joe Bock ends up playing football with the (USFL) Houston Gamblers, where he first meets and plays with future Buffalo Bills quarterback Jim Kelly. To repeat an interesting trivia tidbit, we tossed toward you earlier, Joe Bock was the only person to play professional football as Jim Kelly's teammate on both the Houston Gamblers and the Buffalo Bills.

So, when the Houston basketball and football schedules overlap for the first time, Joe makes arrangements to meet up with his old friend

Ralph Sampson. Joe tells his wife, "Get dressed. We're going out to dinner with the Sampsons."

"You mean I'm going to get to meet Ralph Sampson?" His wife asks.

"Not only that," Joe says, "better yet, we're also going to collect the $28.00 he owes me for that last keg from the Virginia party!"

MOVING ON TO JIM KELLY - The theme of our Joe Bock/Jim Kelly expose is signed football helmets, and the shenanigans related thereto. In that realm, we have two never-before-shared football stories.

FATHER/SON HELMET - This is a classic story involving Jim Kelly that Joe tells at various speaking engagements. Joe has agreed to participate in a silent auction for the Bradford Hospital Charity Golf Tournament in Pennsylvania and has promised to deliver a Jim Kelly signed Buffalo Bills helmet. So, Joe grabs a helmet and leaves Rochester on the afternoon before the day of the tournament with an itinerary of driving to Kelly's house in Buffalo to get the helmet signed and then driving on to Bradford.

Unfortunately, Joe has car trouble along the way and it's after 11 pm by the time he reaches Kelly's house. He drives up, sees that all the lights are out, and momentarily debates whether or not to wake up his friend. Deciding that it is too late Joe leaves and heads for Bradford.

PLAN B - So the next morning Joe wakes up with a dilemma. He's promised this signed helmet to the tournament and his ability to deliver is in serious jeopardy. The wheels in Joe's head are spinning. He does have an autographed picture of Jim Kelly with him and makes the difficult decision that rather than let down the charity auction, he's going to use the autographed picture as a model and try to recreate Kelly's signature on the helmet, knowing that Jim will be okay with it since Joe was in a pinch.

"But I bombed it right off the bat," Joe tells us, *"My 'J' looks more like an '8'. So now I'm thinking what the hell am I gonna do? The tournament starts in half an hour and I'm feeling like I need to save the helmet somehow. I feel like I can't let these people down and you won't believe the idea that creeps into my brain."*

"I started thinking about who amongst Jim Kelly's family and friends might have the two things I need. What would those things be? I need

someone with #1) somewhat shaky handwriting, and #2) a name that starts with a "J".

"Jim Kelly's father's name is Joe and who would know what his signature looks like? So, I decide to try to make it into a father-and-son signed helmet. I turned my butchered 'J' into 'Joe Kelly' and then, on my second attempt got a passable 'Jim Kelly' on the other side of the helmet. It turns out to be one of the biggest hits of the auction. And of course, that helmet would be replaced by an authentic Kelly family version at Jim's earliest convenience."

The next time Joe met up with Jim Kelly, he shared the whole story and Kelly's response was, *"I sure hope you signed my name good!"*

JIM KELLY HELMET 2 ~ Here's our favorite camp story of Joe's. We're going to go to italics for the next several paragraphs and have Joe tell the story.

"One year at my football camp in East Rochester we had obtained a Bills helmet from Super Bowl XXVIII which was the third Super Bowl the Bills played in. We made it a point to be sure that the top kid every year would receive something truly special. I needed to get Jim to sign it so I went to RIT where Jim happened to be simultaneously conducting his own camp. (Note: RIT is a local Rochester college.) Upon arrival I go straight to the main entrance and there is security everywhere. They ask me, 'Who are you here to see,' and I say, 'Jim Kelly.'"

"The guy gets on his walkie talkie, radios Jim Kelly, and tells him that Joe Bock wants to see him. Kelly's response is, 'Ask him if he has any lobster tails,' a reference to the fact that I was the owner and manager of Five-Star Meat and Seafood, a company I had founded in 1984. Jim gets on the radio and says, 'What do you need?' and I say 'One helmet signed.'"

SECRET MEETING ~ *"I can't exactly hear what Jim is saying next. The only part I can make out is 'Meet Field 6. Meet Field 6.' A minute later someone comes in a golf cart and picks me up. We start driving around a winding path through the campus with kids and parents everywhere. We stop at a densely wooded area and I say, 'What are we doing here?'*

JIM TO THE RESCUE ~ *"The cart driver says, 'We have to wait here a minute.' Jim arrives, slaps me up and says, 'Hello, sorry to meet you out here in the woods like we are doing some kind of drug deal or something,* *but if I sign out there where people can see me, I'll start a feeding frenzy and I do not want to do that right now.'"*

This particular meeting spot that Kelly had chosen on the cart path was purposeful because it just happened to be at about the halfway point in the two men's campus locations when Kelly realized that Bock needed him. So, Joe's clandestine deep woods meeting resulted in both survival and success.

JOE BOCK AND JIM KELLY - The relationship between Joe Bock and Jim Kelly is not only unique, it is truly one of a kind. As previously stated, Joe Bock was the only teammate to play pro football with Jim Kelly on both the USFL Houston Gamblers where Kelly started his pro career and the Buffalo Bills where he spent the rest of his legendary career. That component of their relationship is, as we said, truly one of a kind.

In talking about Jim Kelly, Joe has shared with us that not only is Kelly one of his best friends, Kelly is his favorite person and favorite athlete of all time. To hear one pro athlete say that about another struck us as unique from the beginning, but when you hear the conviction with which Joe speaks about Jim, you sense the depth of one man's compassion and respect for another human being.

Thanks for the stories, Joe. We hope they roll on for many years to come.

LET'S JUST CALL IT A VEECK WRECK

Outrageously legendary baseball owner Bill Veeck said that in his lifetime he had to repeat one phrase so often that he made it the title of his autobiography. That phrase, which he used to tell people how to pronounce his name, was *Veeck – As in Wreck* and there is definitely a touch of irony in that title.

Veeck was notorious for his wild and zany promotional gimmicks, and they did not always turn out well. Some were grand slams and some were train wrecks, as in what we'll call "Veeck's wrecks." If you were to see a list of the 10 wildest stunts in the history of baseball, he would probably be associated with about half of them, which is exactly why he is so much fun to write about. A year 2000 article on "The 100 Most Bizarre Sports Moments of the Century" ranked the Eddie Gaedel story, which you'll be reading about soon, as number 1.

Veeck was, at various times, the owner of the St. Louis Browns (currently the Baltimore Orioles franchise), the Cleveland Indians, and the Chicago White Sox. He was an absolutely wild spirit and the last owner to purchase a baseball franchise without an independent fortune. Veeck came up with publicity stunts that were never rivaled in the history of the game. Furthermore, in this conservative, politically correct modern-day era, many of the antics he was able to pursue will never again be possible. Here are some highlights.

EDDIE GAEDEL ~ Bill Veeck's first great stunt resulted in a player who, in the *Baseball Encyclopedia,* will remain forever tied for first place with an on-base percentage of 100%. As the owner of the St. Louis Browns during the 1940's, Veeck always played second fiddle to the cross-town St. Louis Cardinals and constantly resorted to his own diverse devices to create PR gimmicks hoping to increase attendance.

So, let's go back to the late summer of 1941 and bask in the St. Louis sunshine. The fields are green, the national pastime is in full swing, and the Pearl Harbor air raid sirens have not yet begun to ring. Bill Veeck announces that on August 19, any St. Louis baseball fans who come to the Browns' game are guaranteed to witness something they have never seen before.

The showman Veeck certainly delivers on his promise. As the Browns come up to bat in the bottom of the first inning, the PA announcer stuns the audience with the news that the Browns leadoff man is being replaced by a pinch hitter. Resonating through the stadium is the question of, "Why in the world would they do this?"

These resonations turn into a thunderous applause when Eddie Gaedel, a 3' 8" midget, determinedly departs the dugout and menacingly meanders toward home plate, wearing the uniform number 1/8 on his back. While Veeck's scruples are suspect, his strategy is sound. As anticipated, Gaedel walks on four pitches, leisurely strolls towards first base, stopping on two occasions to bow and acknowledge the applause of the crowd.

Upon reaching first, Gaedel takes that giant step to board the base. When you're only 3' 8", that three-inch-high base is a steeper climb than you might suspect. Upon ascending his figurative Mt. Everest, Gaedel balances himself, and pirouettes through four 90° angle rotations. After a pinch runner is announced to the crowd, Gaedel leaves first base and proudly prances back to the dugout amidst one of the most riotous revelries in St. Louis sports history.

Not unexpectedly, Gaedel is banned from baseball the next day. The basis of the ban is that Veeck has violated the official rule of committing an act "not in the best interest of the game." Sometimes people just can't take a joke.

But none of that changes one fact. For all of eternity, Eddie Gaedel's name will be forever documented in the *Baseball Encyclopedia* as one of the few players who reached base in 100% of his official plate appearances.

Another unique irony of the Eddie Gaedel story is the surprising saga of his signature value. Due to its rarity, Eddie Gaedel's autograph is worth more than Babe Ruth's. No foolin'. While this may initially seem shocking, it's really just a result of the economic concept of supply and demand. Ruth was an outgoing affable celebrity who was constantly being asked for his autograph and always did his best to oblige.

At the time who would have ever thought that Gaedel's autograph would have been worth much and even if you had a hunch it might be worth getting, how would you even go about seeking it out? So the result is that, while there are thousands of Babe Ruth autographs in circulation, there are only a few dozen of Eddie Gaedel's, hence the surprising comparative values.

Let's add an aspect of American media history connectivity to this 1941 Gaedel thread. Just four years before, in 1937, the country had seen the almost simultaneous movie releases of both *Snow White and the Seven Dwarfs* from Disney and *The Wizard of Oz* featuring the Munchkins, so the concept of little people was very much in the American psyche at the time.

We are saving Veeck's greatest hit, or what we would more accurately describe as his greatest miss, for our book's crescendo. In referring back to the aforementioned article on "The 100 Most Bizarre Sports Moments of the Century," this one came in at number 5. That being said, we would personally flip flop those ratings so we are saving what we consider to be number 1 for our grand finale.

However, before we get to the most notorious Veeck story of all time, please allow us to share with you brief versions of some of its predecessors. Keeping all of this mess in perspective, these consecutive stories manage to convey the degree to which Bill Veeck disrupted and influenced the game of baseball without ever having won a championship.

Ironically in a game played just five days after the Eddie Gaedel extravaganza, Veeck had already received approval for an event he had billed as "Grandstand Managers Night" during which the fans would be allowed to vote on various strategic decisions by holding up placards.

GRANDSTAND MANAGERS NIGHT ~ One birthright of every baseball fan is questioning the managerial decisions of your team when things go wrong. Ever the showman, Bill Veeck came up with an interesting ploy to combat this problem in a game his St. Louis Browns played against the Philadelphia Athletics on August 24, 1941.

Here's how "Grandstand Managers Night" worked. In a designated section of the grandstand, fans were provided with placards that had the word "YES" on one side and "NO" on the other. At strategically appropriate times where yes/no decisions were in order, the game was briefly paused and the fans were genuinely allowed the opportunity to dictate the Browns' play on the field by a majority vote.

Examples of the types of situations where the fans could vote yea or nay included the following.

- Should the team send up a pitch hitter?
- Should the infield play in or play deep?
- Should the pitcher be taken out?

The Browns, who did not have a very good team, actually won the game 5-3. It's therefore surprising that Veeck did not make Grandstand

Managers Night a more frequent occurrence. But as history confirms this was a one-time event.

MORE MIDGET MANIA ~ While his major league career consisted of just the one plate appearance, Eddie Gaedel was involved with other Major League Baseball games. After becoming owner of the Chicago White Sox in 1959, Bill Veeck hired Gaedel and three other midgets to dress up as Martian spacemen and gift the White Sox players with ray guns.

Whether or not the players were offered the opportunity to return fire is not historically documented. When the players asked Gaedel if he wanted to meet with the owner, Gaedel was quoted as saying, "I don't want to be taken to your leader. I've already met him."

In 1961 Veeck again hired several midgets, including Gaedel, as vendors. Can you guess the reason why? Veeck cited this move as an attempt to improve the overall experience of the fans at his games. Midget vendors, he reasoned, would not block the view of the spectators. The man thought of everything.

WHITE SOX '70's STUNTS ~ During this decade, Bill Veeck continued to institute innovations which ranged from sterling successes to middle-of-the road mediocrities to decimating disasters. We'll start with the successes and work our way down to the disasters because those are actually much more fun.

EXPLODING SCOREBOARD ~ Comiskey Park in Chicago had professional sports' first scoreboard to display special effects and exploding fireworks. Nowadays, there's not a scoreboard around that doesn't come with some bells and whistles. So bravo, Bill. This one was a stroke of genius on your part. This innovation became universal.

Veeck was also the first to have picnic areas installed within the confines of a ballpark. While not a universal stadium accoutrement, many major league ballparks have copied this concept.

MIDDLE OF THE ROAD ~ Comiskey also had an outdoor shower in the centerfield bleachers. So if you were baking in the sun on a hot Chicago summer day, and we're of a mind to do so, you had the opportunity to cool off with a centerfield shower. An unfortunate reality of the shower scenario was that it attracted many more beer bellies than bikini babes.

CALL THE POLICE ~ Veeck could have, and perhaps should have, been arrested for many of his shenanigans but he absolutely deserved a visit from the fashion police for the alternate uniforms he conceived for the White Sox in the late 1970's. On designated days during games in the summer, the team had an alternate set of home uniforms that featured v-neck jerseys and two questionable pant options.

One option featured short pants (players loved sliding in these) and the other featured three-quarter length pants (hey dude, love the Capris). So if you're looking for Veeck to outdo his faux pas of having men take the field in women's clothing, not to worry, he won't disappoint you. Prepare yourself for the big enchilada of promotional extravaganzas gone horribly awry.

DISCO DEMOLITION NIGHT ~ If you were reviewing the nominees for the most ill-conceived sports promotion of all time, Disco Demolition Night would certainly be amongst those nominations and we would be hard pressed to not just declare it the outright winner. In our hypothetical award show, the group of three men who would have to come forward, reluctantly, to accept the award would be Chicago White Sox owner Bill Veeck; his son, promotions manager Mike Veeck; and Chicago radio personality Steve Dahl.

This infamous event took place on July 12, 1979 in between games of a double header between the White Sox and the Detroit Tigers. Disco music rode the crest of a wave of popularity in America for much of the 1970's. John Travolta striking an arm-extended pose on the cover of the *Saturday Night Fever* album was perhaps the most iconic visual image of the movement and a stream of hits from artists like the Bee Gees, Donna Summer, and the Village People provided the audio soundtrack. And while disco obviously had its supporters there was always an undercurrent of stark opposition to the genre.

Having lived it, here is our best explanation of what was different about disco. In most cases if you don't like a genre of music you simply ignore it. However, disco somehow managed to grate upon its non-fans to the point where those non-fans couldn't just ignore it, they felt compelled to passionately strike out against it.

So, when the popularity of disco finally began to fade in the late 70's the haters rejoiced like their team had just won the World Series, to use a baseball analogy apropos for this article. And therein lies the basis for what enabled Disco Demolition Night to turn into such an ugly disaster. It was a celebration of hatred rather than a salute to something positive. At any rate, let us tell you how it all went down.

At the time Steve Dahl was a disc jockey for the Chicago rock radio station WLUP-FM 98 and he collaborated with Bill Veeck and his son Mike Veeck on this promotion whereby fans who surrendered their old disco records could buy a ticket for the double header for just 98 cents (based upon the station's position on the radio dial). And you might have considered it a triple header because everyone in attendance would also get to cheer on the destruction of the "surrendered" disco records which were scheduled to be literally blown up in between games. How about a little "Play That Funky Music, White Boy" to set the mood?

Here are the pertinent numbers for the event. The seating capacity of Comiskey Park was about 45,000. Attendance the previous night had been 15,000 and they are hoping to get 20,000 for the promotion. Security has been hired to deal with 35,000 just in case. The game sells out which initially seems to be good news but Comiskey is on the south side of Chicago which may have been symbolically important because things start to go south rapidly when at least 20,000 ticketless fans show up outside the stadium looking for ways to sneak in.

Unprepared for such an event, stadium security is overmatched and thousands of people manage to scale fences or leap turnstiles to gain entrance. Estimates as to how many people actually fill the stadium range as high as 70,000, twice the amount that security has been prepared to handle. This was clearly the recipe for a "Disco Inferno."

We have opted to use a timeline format to detail the events of the evening.

5:00 ~ The gates open and upon entry record-bearing attendees are asked to place their vinyl discs in a 5-foot-square box which, if you haven't figured this out already, is way too small to accomplish its desired task of collecting all the disco records which will be brought to the game tonight. Once the box overflows many fans just carry the records to their seats.

5:30 ~ Mike Veeck receives word that thousands of people are trying to get in without tickets.

5:38 ~ Veeck decides to send most of the available security to the perimeter of the stadium to contain would-be gate crashers, leaving security around the field itself undermanned.

6:00 ~ The crowd is driven into its first frenzy when local sex kitten model Lorelei Shark struts to the mound to throw out the first pitch. Lorelei's impressive resumé includes appearances in both *Playboy* and *Playgirl* magazines, clearly demonstrating her range of appeal. She was also on the *Laugh In* TV show and she is the anonymous owner of the set of lips that adorn the iconic movie poster for *The Rocky Horror Picture Show*. On a less positive note, dozens of banners with negative slogans like "Disco Sucks" are seen hanging throughout the stadium.

6:05 ~ Game 1 begins.

6:48 ~ Commentators note the first examples of foreign objects being tossed onto the field. They go on to say that many of the objects are vinyl records being thrown as frisbee discs, some of which, depending on their angle of flight, actually embed themselves in the grass surface leaving a semi-circle protruding from the ground. If you ever find yourself in a position where it matters, because they are heavier and the hole is smaller, full-length albums make better frisbees than 45's.

6:55 ~ Umpires stop the game for the first of several times to allow the field crew to collect debris which fans have thrown onto the field. Veteran Detroit Tigers player Rusty Staub tells his teammates to wear their batting helmets while playing positions in the field.

7:25 ~ The on-site Chicago news crew from WGN notes that there are groups of mainly "music people," not baseball fans, wandering throughout the park clearly disinterested in the game.

7:45 ~ White Sox broadcasters, Harry Caray and Jimmy Piersall, comment over the air that the smell of marijuana has drifted into the press box. Side note on this one – we tend to trust Piersall's judgment on gauging this aroma because the most notable event of his own major league career was that when he hit his 100th home run he ran the bases backwards; in the correct order, but backwards.

8:16 ~ Game 1 ends with Detroit prevailing by a score of 4-1.

8:28 ~ Ken Kravec, White Sox starting pitcher for game 2, takes the mound to warm up.

8:30 ~ Radio personality Steve Dahl is driven onto the field in a jeep wearing army fatigues and a helmet accompanied by the aforementioned model Lorelei. The jeep circles the stadium one time with Dahl and Lorelei leading the crowd in a chant of "Disco Sucks." The jeep proceeds to center field where the box of disco records awaits.

8:35 ~ Specifics on what went wrong with the pyrotechnics piece of the event are not clearly available but the result of the explosion is the creation of a crater in center field.

8:36 ~ Many legitimate fans, feeling things have gotten out of control, head for the gates which have mostly been locked by Veeck to avoid more unwanted intruders. The first of 5000-7000 "illegitimate" fans begin pouring onto the field.

8:37 ~ Pitcher Ken Kravec decides his survival is more important than warming up and sprints toward the dugout.

8:40 ~ The first person is sighted shimmying up the right field foul pole.

8:41 ~ The first person is sighted shimmying up the left field foul pole.

8:45 ~ If you are still following the Lorelei thread she is thrown into the jeep and driven away to safety.

8:47 ~ The bases at first and third are pulled from the ground never to be seen again.

8:48 ~ Ditto, second base.

8:50 ~ While ironically the scoreboard is flashing "Please Return to Your Seats" several hundred people are dancing around the fire that has been lit in center field to burn the remnants of the vinyl records in the crater. Popcorn boxes and beer cups are thrown in to fuel the fire. The soundtrack to this crazy scenario is that the PA is now playing "Take Me

Out to the Ballgame." Perhaps a better choice would have been "Burn, Baby, Burn, Disco Inferno."

9:08 ~ Chicago police in full riot gear march onto the field finally ending the chaos. Most of the crowd hastily disperses. Thirty-nine people who feel like staying for the after party is a good idea are arrested for disorderly conduct.

At this point the grounds crew begins cleanup efforts with Veeck somehow thinking that Game 2 might actually still be played. Detroit Tigers manager, Sparky Anderson, was later quoted as saying, "I might have allowed my players to go to center field and join in the marshmallow roast but there is not a chance in hell that I would have allowed them to play baseball on that field."

Amidst the chaos American League president, Lee MacPhail, is being updated on a story he certainly never thought he would hear. MacPhail calls for the official cancellation of Game 2. The following day, faulting Chicago's abhorred handling of the entire event, he forfeits the game to Detroit.

Only four games have been forfeited in American League history and this was the last. On his radio show the next morning Steve Dahl said, "I never thought that I, a stupid disc jockey, could draw 70,000 people to a disco demolition. Unfortunately, some of our followers got a little carried away. Hey, the original festival of peace, love, and music was almost a decade ago; maybe Disco Demolition Night was the Woodstock these kids never had."

Part of Dahl's legacy is that he will forever be attached to one of the most bizarre stories in the history of baseball and of the three men involved in the promotion he definitely survived the debacle in the best shape. He skyrocketed to local fame on the Chicago radio scene and hosted a popular radio show into the 2010's.

Bill Veeck was already nearing the end of a storied career in baseball. In 1981 he sold the White Sox and was never officially involved in baseball again before passing away in 1986.

His son, Mike Veeck claimed that Disco Demolition Night caused him to be subsequently blackballed in the baseball world, but he did successfully rebound. He became the owner of the independent St. Paul Saints and the minor league Charleston River Dogs.

As for Lorelei, her whereabouts are currently unknown.

ABOUT THE AUTHORS

We have a rather unique back story, most of which is set in upstate New York. We met on the first day of high school, brought together by the merger of two neighboring school districts. We ended up dating for all four years of high school, then went to different colleges and, as fate would have it, we ended up not seeing each other again for literally 40 years.

Tim's mom passed away in late 2012 and Deb heard about it through the grapevine in Virginia Beach where she was teaching. She sent him a sympathy card, he wrote back, one thing led to another and Tim ended up coming down to Virginia Beach in June of 2013 to pick Deb up after her school year ended and bringing her back to New York.

The thing Deb remembers most from that courtship period when she was in Virginia, but longing to be back in New York, was that every day at school when she went to her mailbox, there was an envelope from Tim. And each one contained an original letter Deb had written to him 40 years ago. He had saved every one. His go-to line regarding that part of the story is to say, "Yeah, it took me a long time to play those cards!" Sometimes the best things in life are worth waiting for.

We got engaged on Deb's mother's birthday (December 4, 2014) and we got married on Tim's mother's birthday (June 12, 2015). Because we both have Native American ancestry, we had the ceremony performed at the Ganondagan Historic Site by the Native American leader there, as well as a former student of Tim's.

So how did we get into this writing gig? Well, as fate would have it, we happen to live right next door to the newspaper office in our town. After hearing some of our stories, the publisher of the paper Chris Carosa suggested we write something for the paper. So we started by telling the personal story of our relationship and we haven't stopped writing since. Currently our weekly feature comprises the entire back page of the *Mendon-Honeoye Falls-Lima Sentinel*.

We write about an eclectic variety of topics including music, sports, travel and human interest. Our publisher had been encouraging us to write a book for some time now and we had been waiting for a topic to emerge about which we felt we could apply our own irreverent twist. That project came to fruition with the publication of our first book *The Beatles, The Bible & Manson: Reflecting Back with 50 Years of Perspective* in the summer of 2019.

If you enjoyed this second book of ours, please seek out our first; it's a killer.